# AQUATLANTIC

GIORGIO CARPINTERI

*Translated by Jamie Richards*

FANTAGRAPHICS

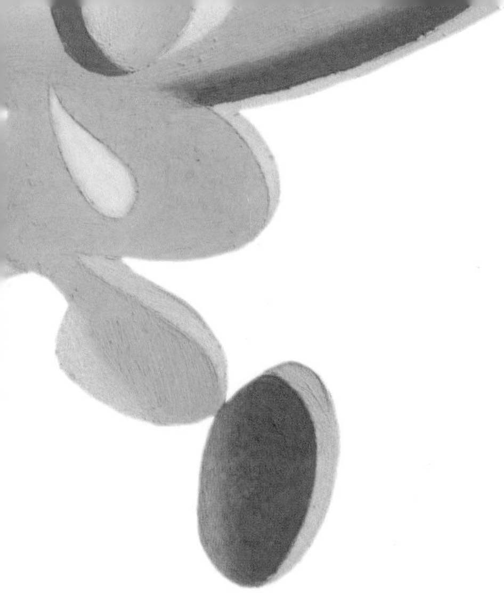

FANTAGRAPHICS BOOKS INC.
7563 Lake City Way Northeast
Seattle, Washington, 98115 USA
WWW.FANTAGRAPHICS.COM

EDITOR & ASSOCIATE PUBLISHER: Eric Reynolds
TRANSLATED FROM ITALIAN BY: Jamie Richards
GRAPHIC DESIGN: Chelsea Wirtz
PRODUCTION: Paul Baresh
PUBLISHER: Gary Groth



Images of the puffer fish sand mandala are taken from the BBC documentary series *Life Story Earth: Puffer Fish Constructs a Masterpiece of Love.*

ISBN: 978-1-68396-351-6
LIBRARY OF CONGRESS CONTROL NUMBER: 2020934856

FIRST PRINTING: September 2020
PRINTED IN CHINA

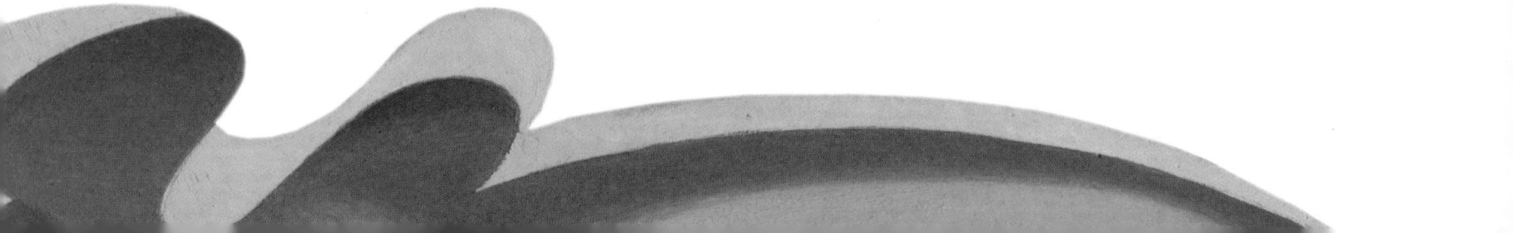

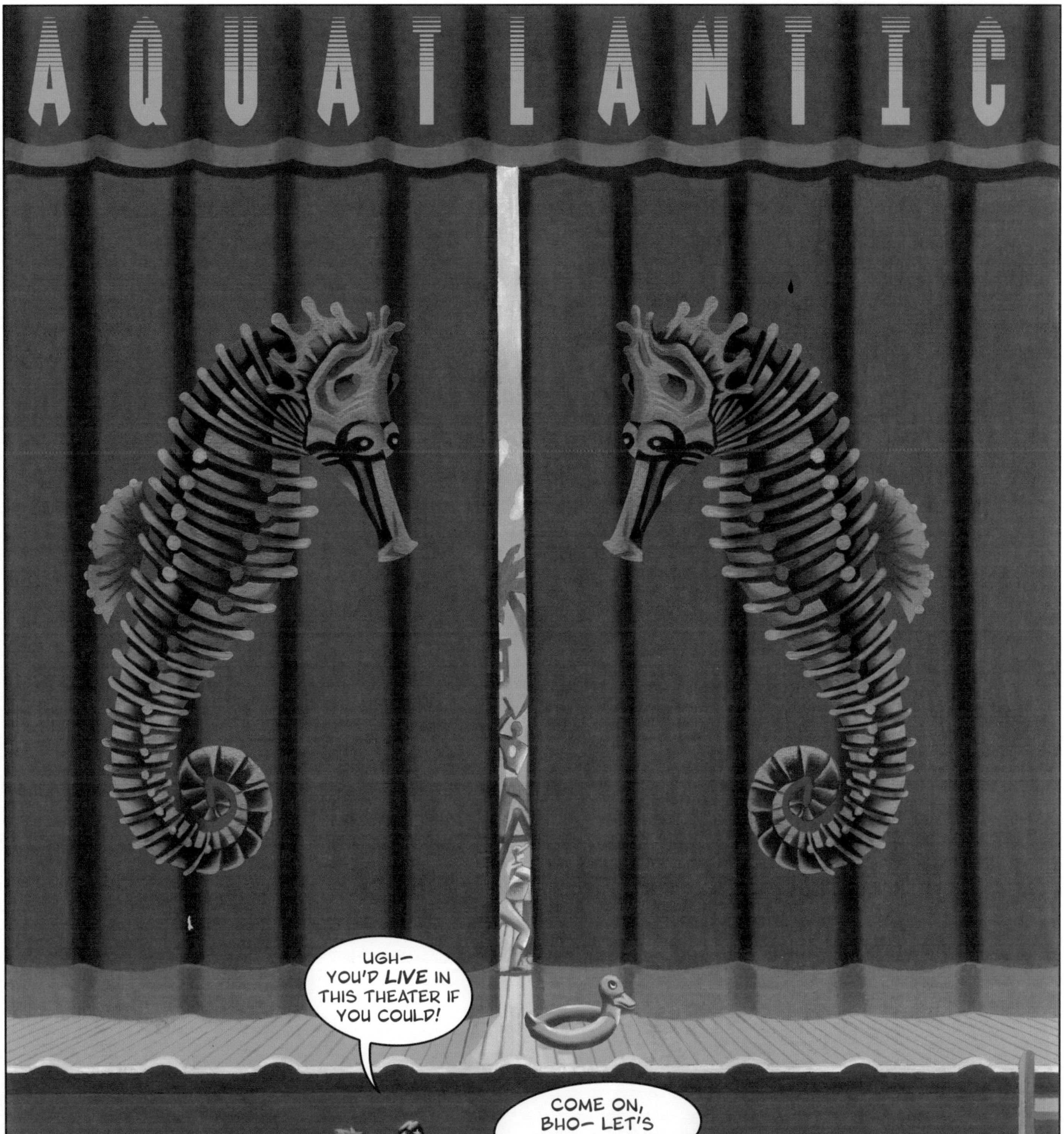
AQUATLANTIC
UGH— YOU'D LIVE IN THIS THEATER IF YOU COULD!
COME ON, BHO— LET'S TAKE A WALK.

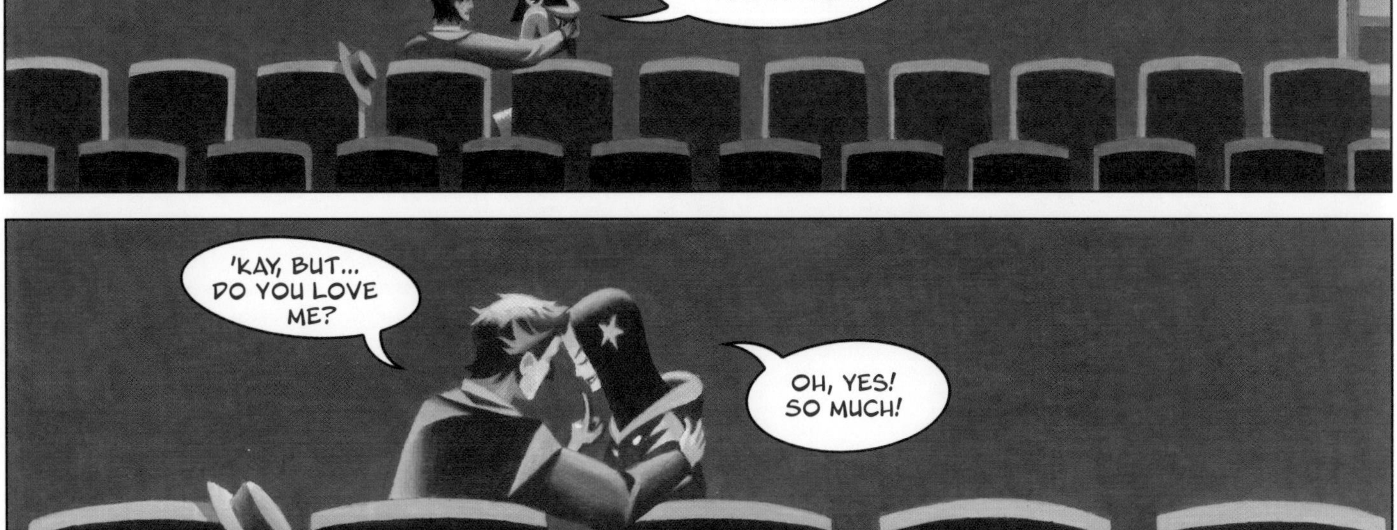
'KAY, BUT... DO YOU LOVE ME?
OH, YES! SO MUCH!

Aquatlantic. 07-06-00001
Dear Maestro, You taught me that when I'm unhappy, I should write down my reflections, my thoughts.

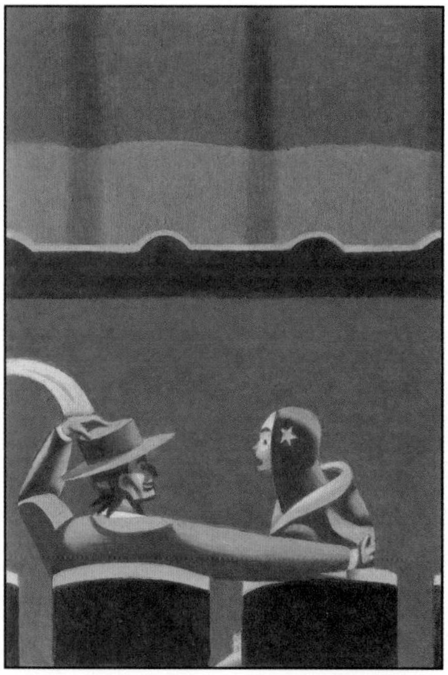

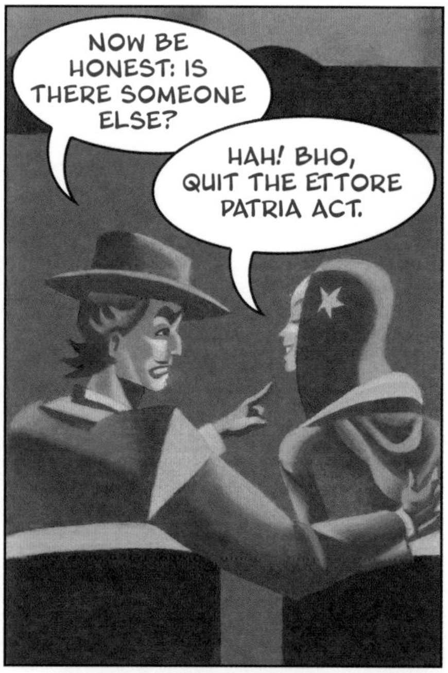
NOW BE HONEST: IS THERE SOMEONE ELSE?
HAH! BHO, QUIT THE ETTORE PATRIA ACT.

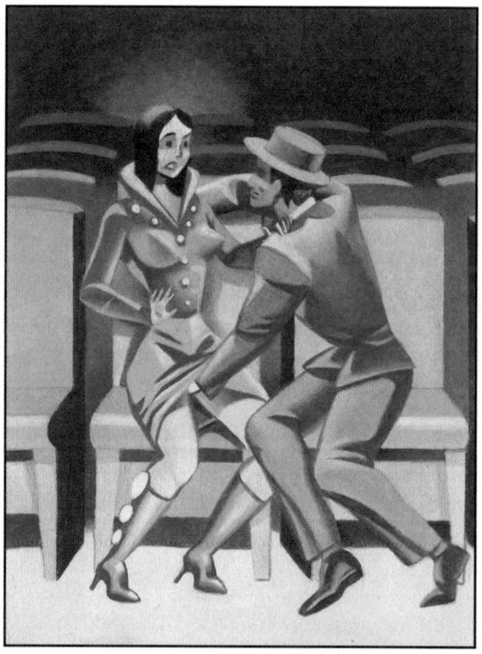

I told you what I did to Stella, but you didn't say a word.

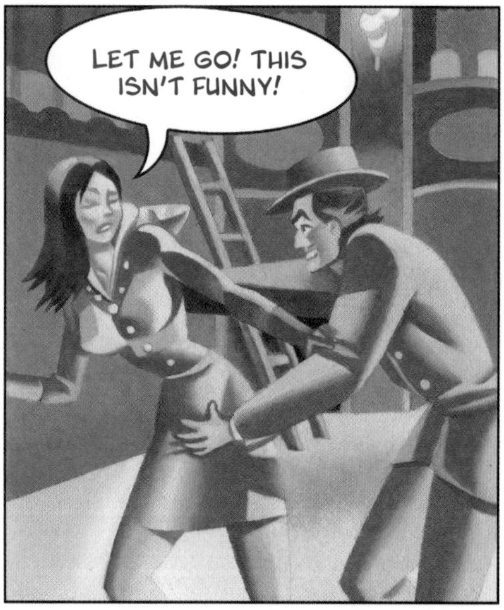
LET ME GO! THIS ISN'T FUNNY!

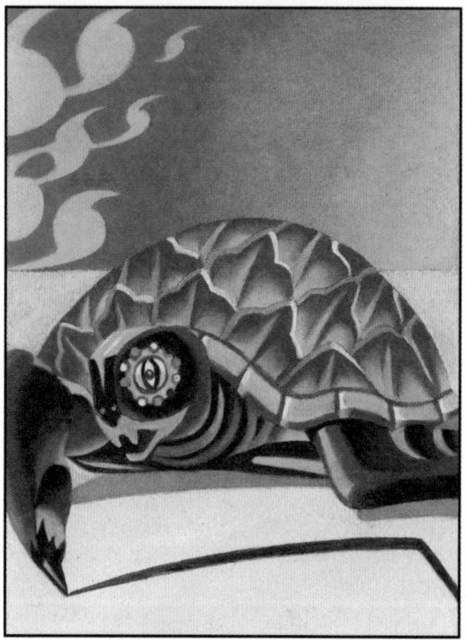

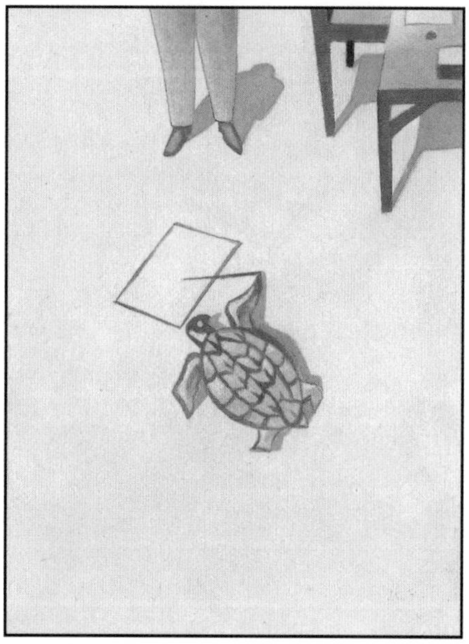

You just drew a rectangle and a line on the floor.

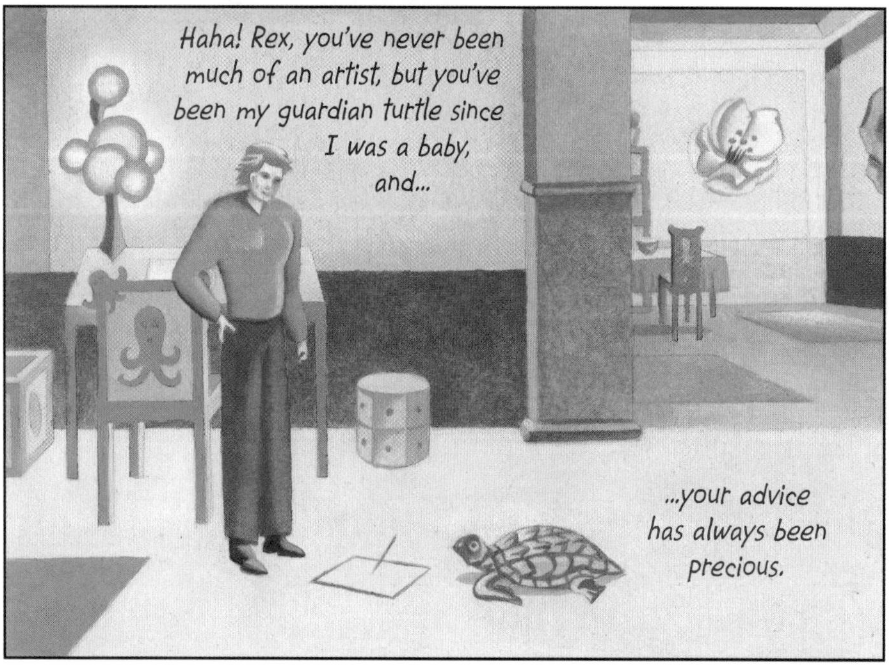
Haha! Rex, you've never been much of an artist, but you've been my guardian turtle since I was a baby, and...
...your advice has always been precious.

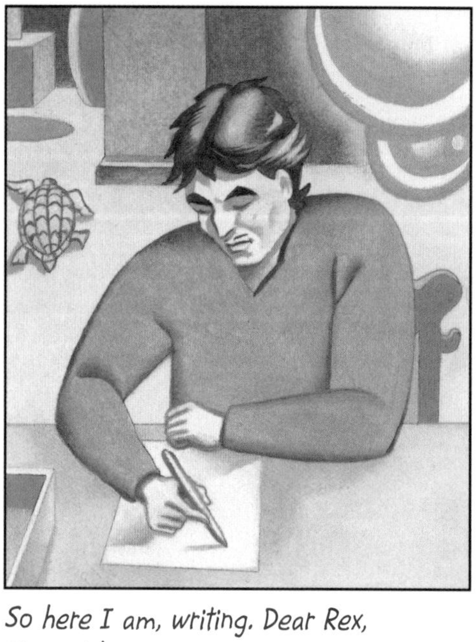

So here I am, writing. Dear Rex, I'm not happy.

*I rise up in song every day, but am distracted by a disturbing recurring dream.*

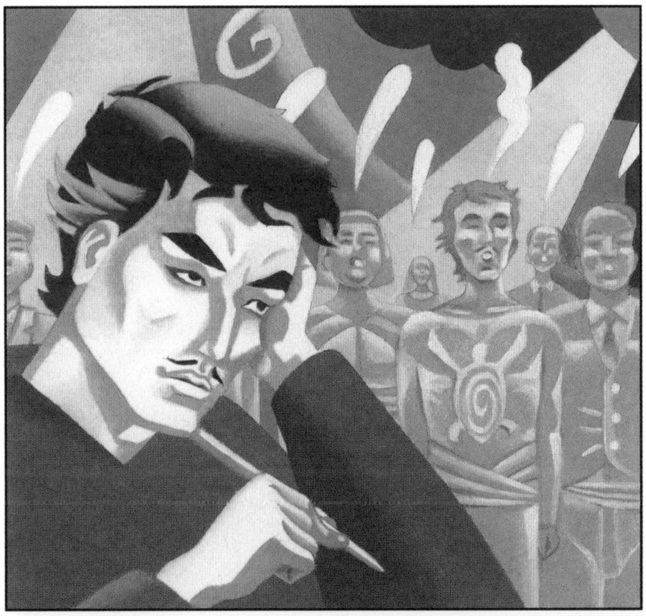

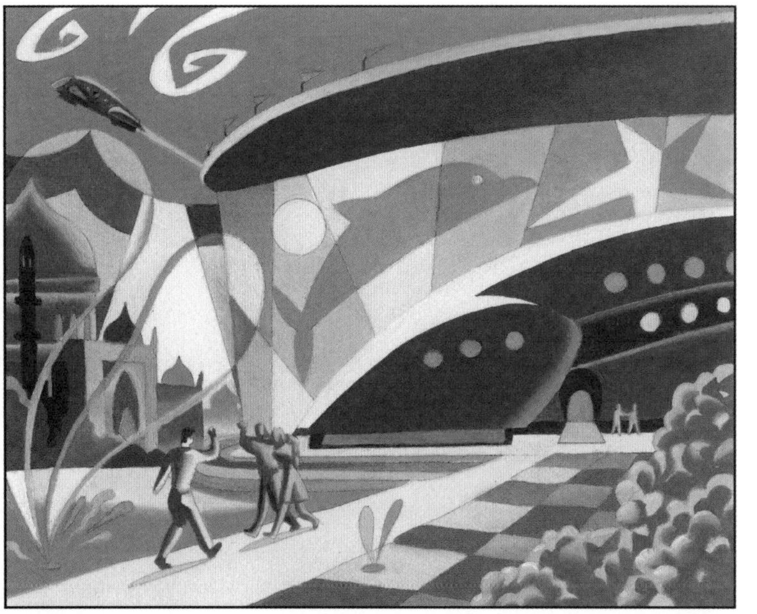

*So today I worked up the nerve to go and talk to my old friend, Lah– the tall one.*

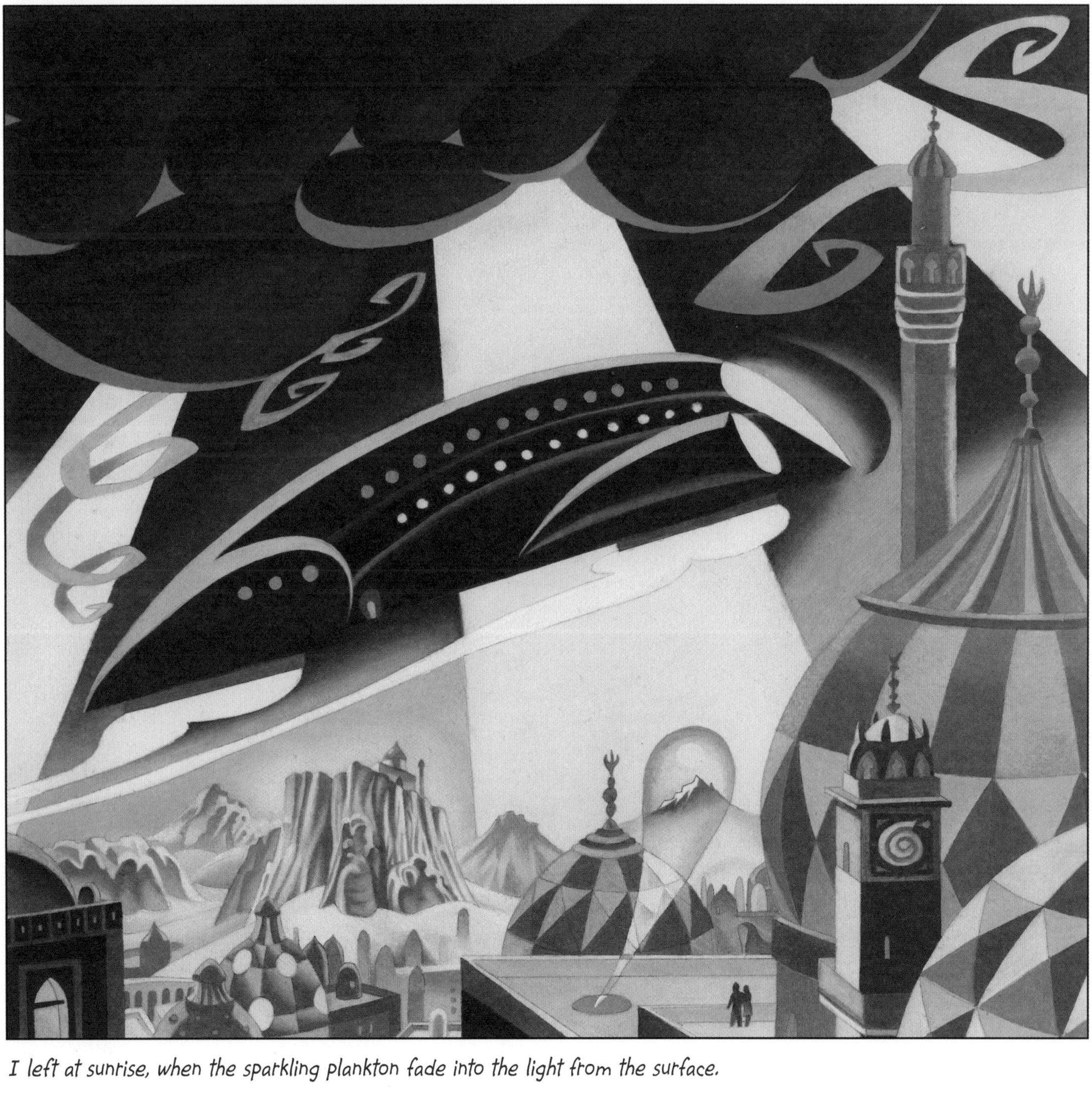

*I left at sunrise, when the sparkling plankton fade into the light from the surface.*

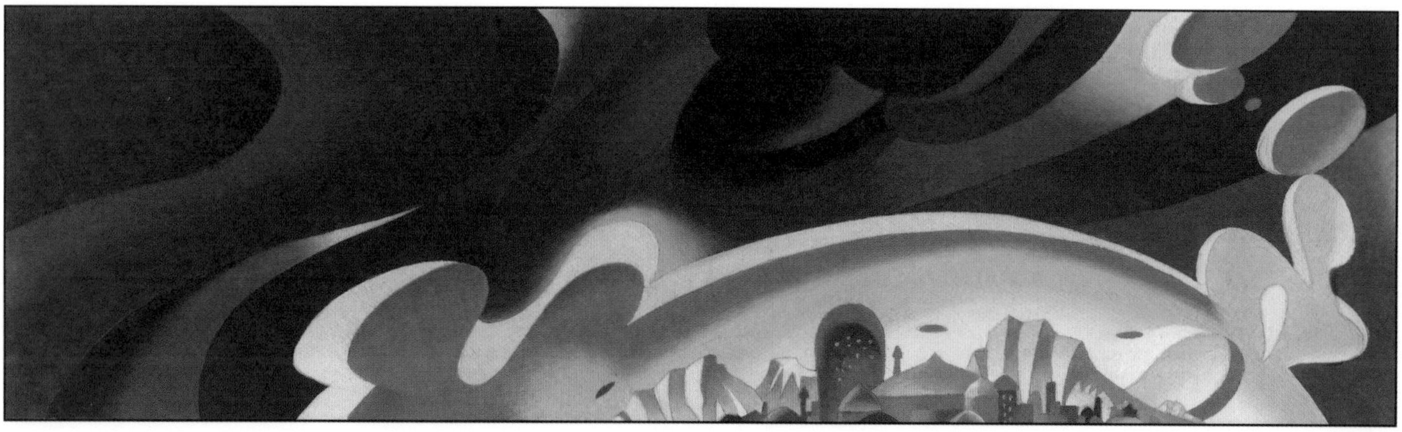

A spark of happiness flashed through me, as I took in Aquatlantic through the window...

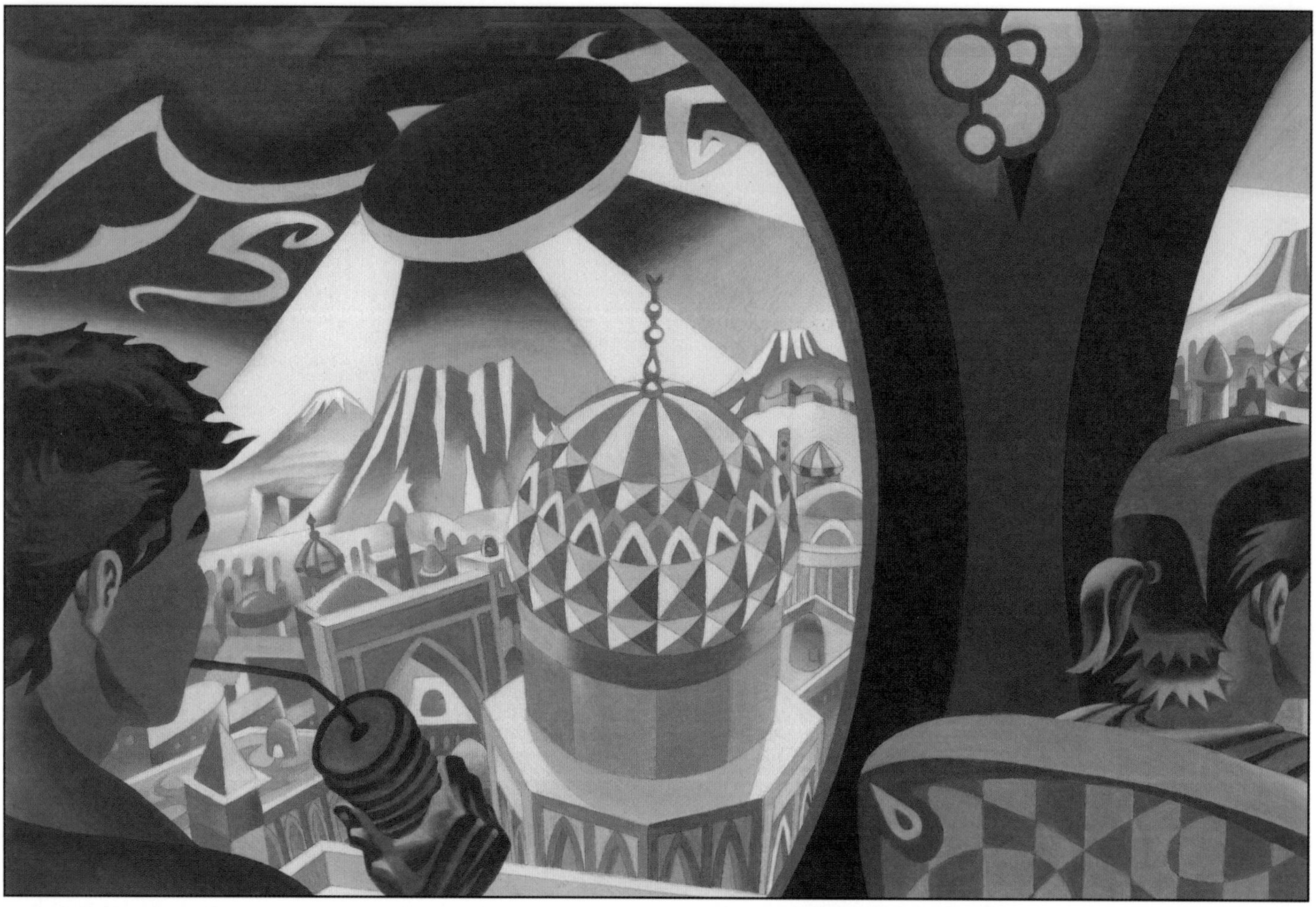

... but quickly dimmed at the thought that I couldn't really be honest with my friend.

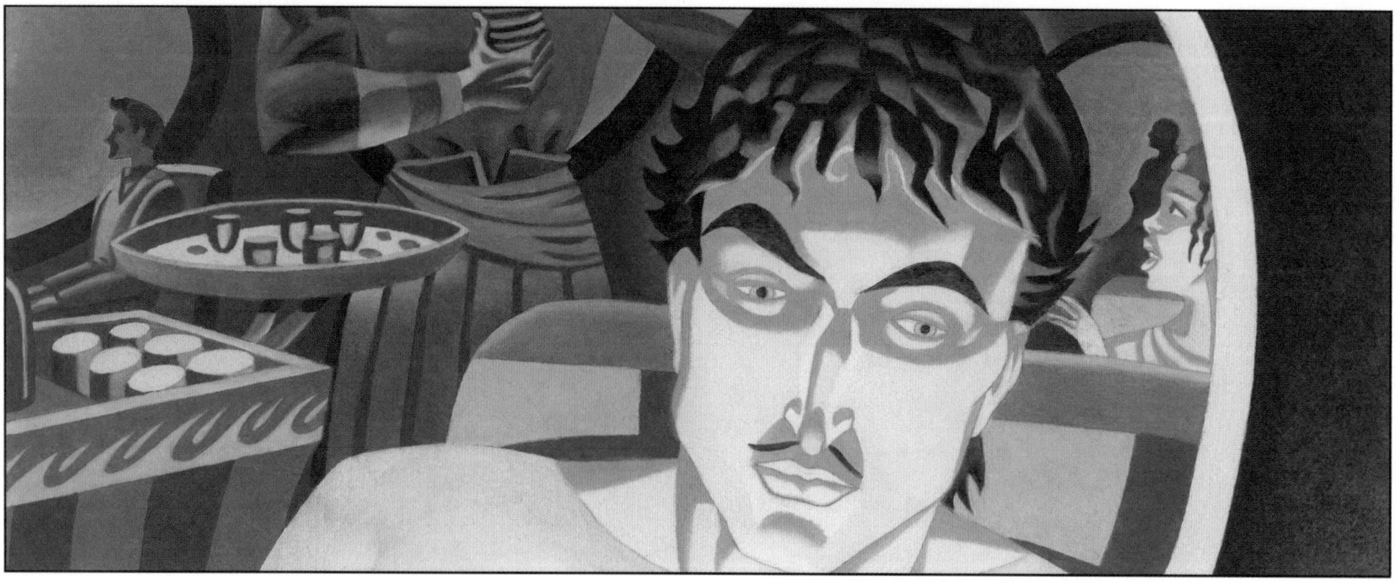

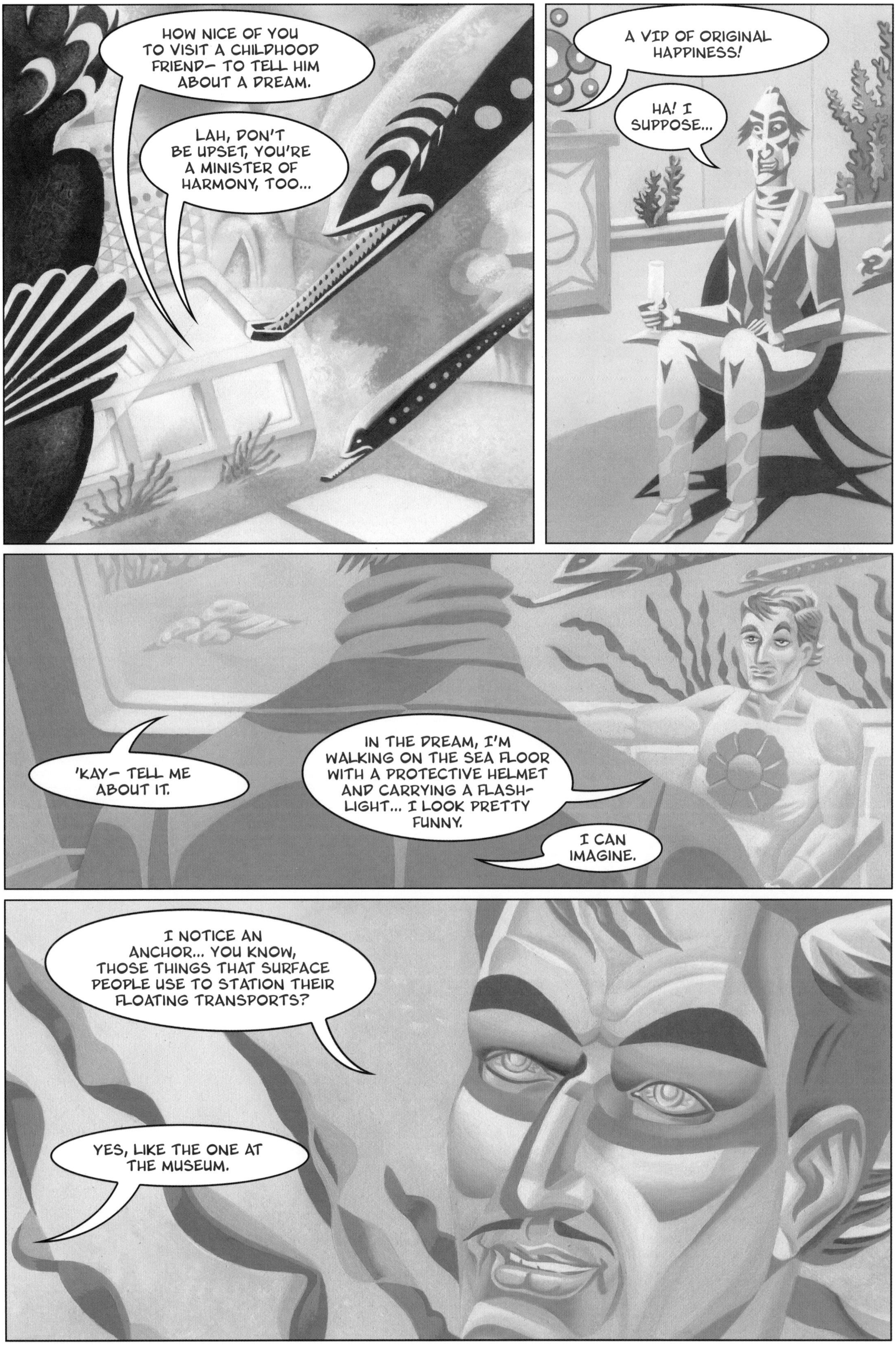
HOW NICE OF YOU TO VISIT A CHILDHOOD FRIEND— TO TELL HIM ABOUT A DREAM.
LAH, DON'T BE UPSET, YOU'RE A MINISTER OF HARMONY, TOO...
A VIP OF ORIGINAL HAPPINESS!
HA! I SUPPOSE...
'KAY— TELL ME ABOUT IT.
IN THE DREAM, I'M WALKING ON THE SEA FLOOR WITH A PROTECTIVE HELMET AND CARRYING A FLASH-LIGHT... I LOOK PRETTY FUNNY.
I CAN IMAGINE.
I NOTICE AN ANCHOR... YOU KNOW, THOSE THINGS THAT SURFACE PEOPLE USE TO STATION THEIR FLOATING TRANSPORTS?
YES, LIKE THE ONE AT THE MUSEUM.

AS I WALK OVER TO THE ANCHOR, I KEEP REPEATING A RHYME IN MY HEAD THAT GOES SOMETHING LIKE:
ONE,
TWO,
THREE...
FOOL PLUS IDIOT PLUS DUNCE EQUALS ME!

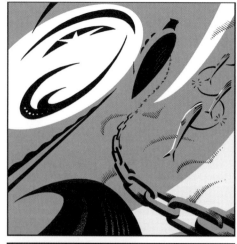

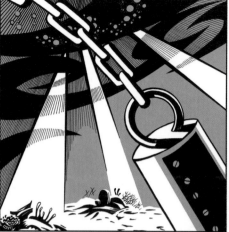

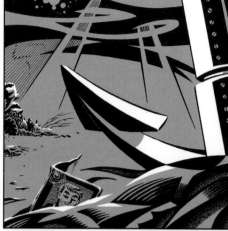

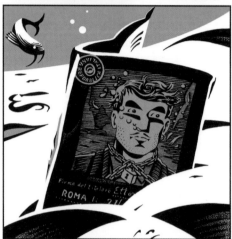

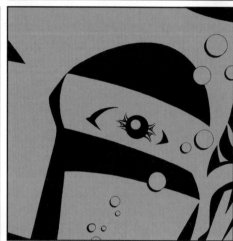

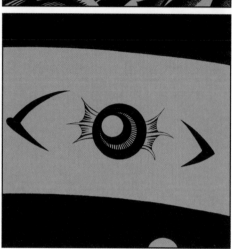

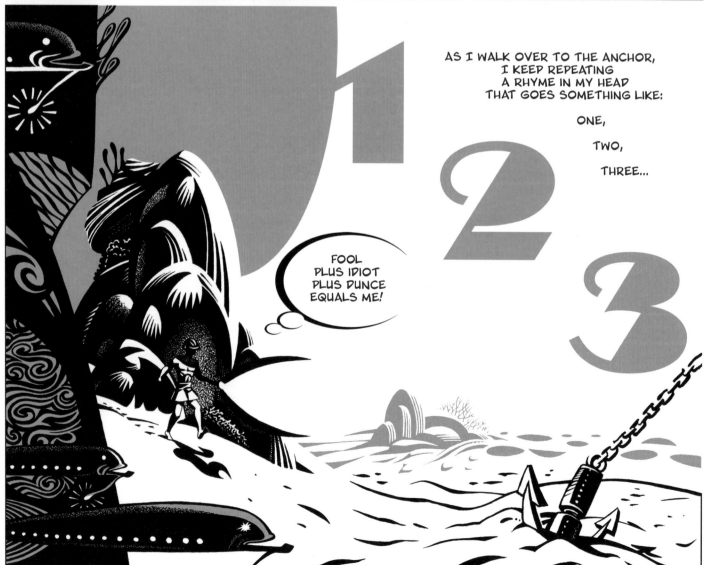

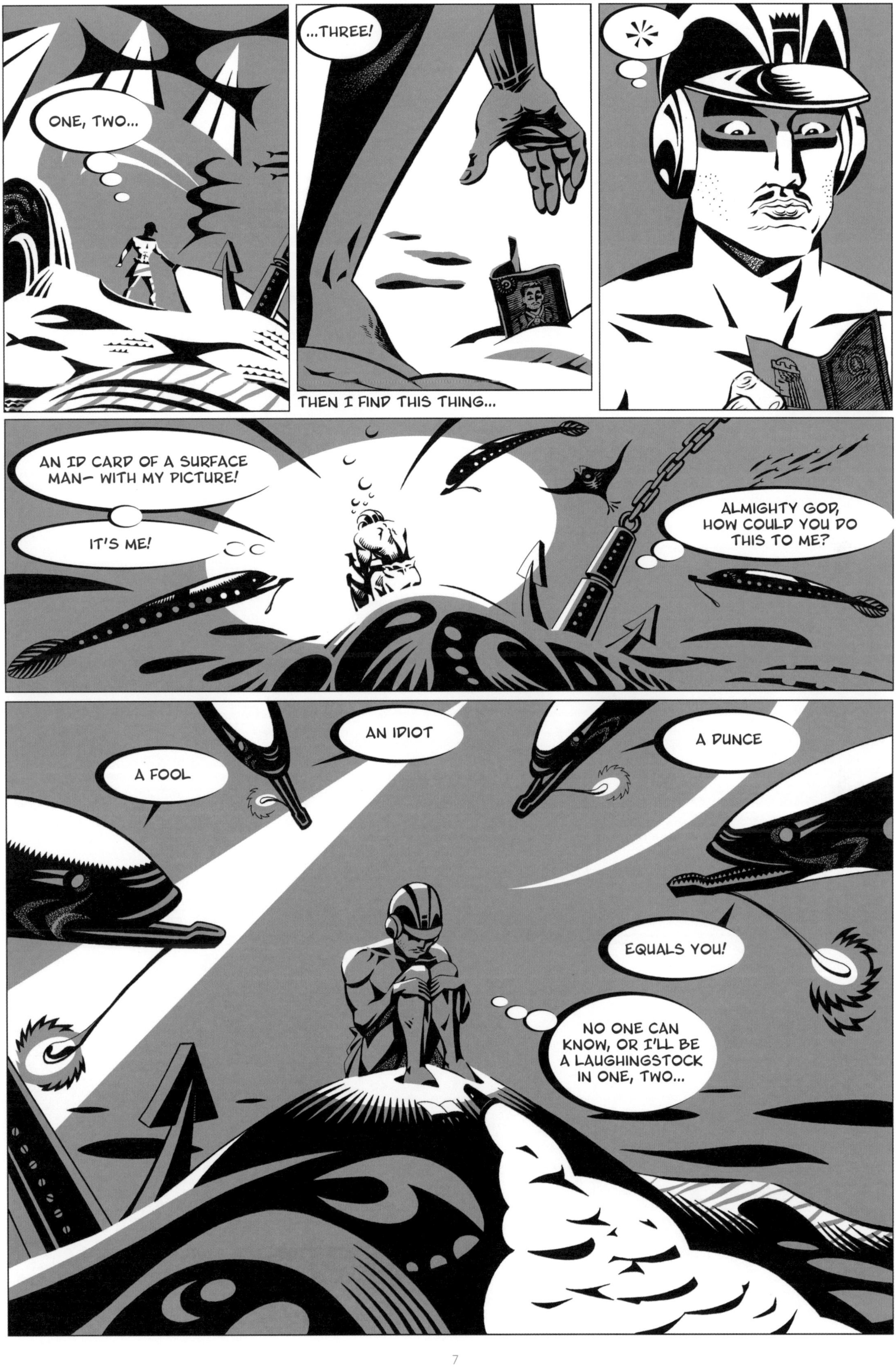
ONE, TWO...
...THREE!
THEN I FIND THIS THING...
*!*
AN ID CARD OF A SURFACE MAN— WITH MY PICTURE!
IT'S ME!
ALMIGHTY GOD, HOW COULD YOU DO THIS TO ME?
A FOOL
AN IDIOT
A DUNCE
EQUALS YOU!
NO ONE CAN KNOW, OR I'LL BE A LAUGHINGSTOCK IN ONE, TWO...

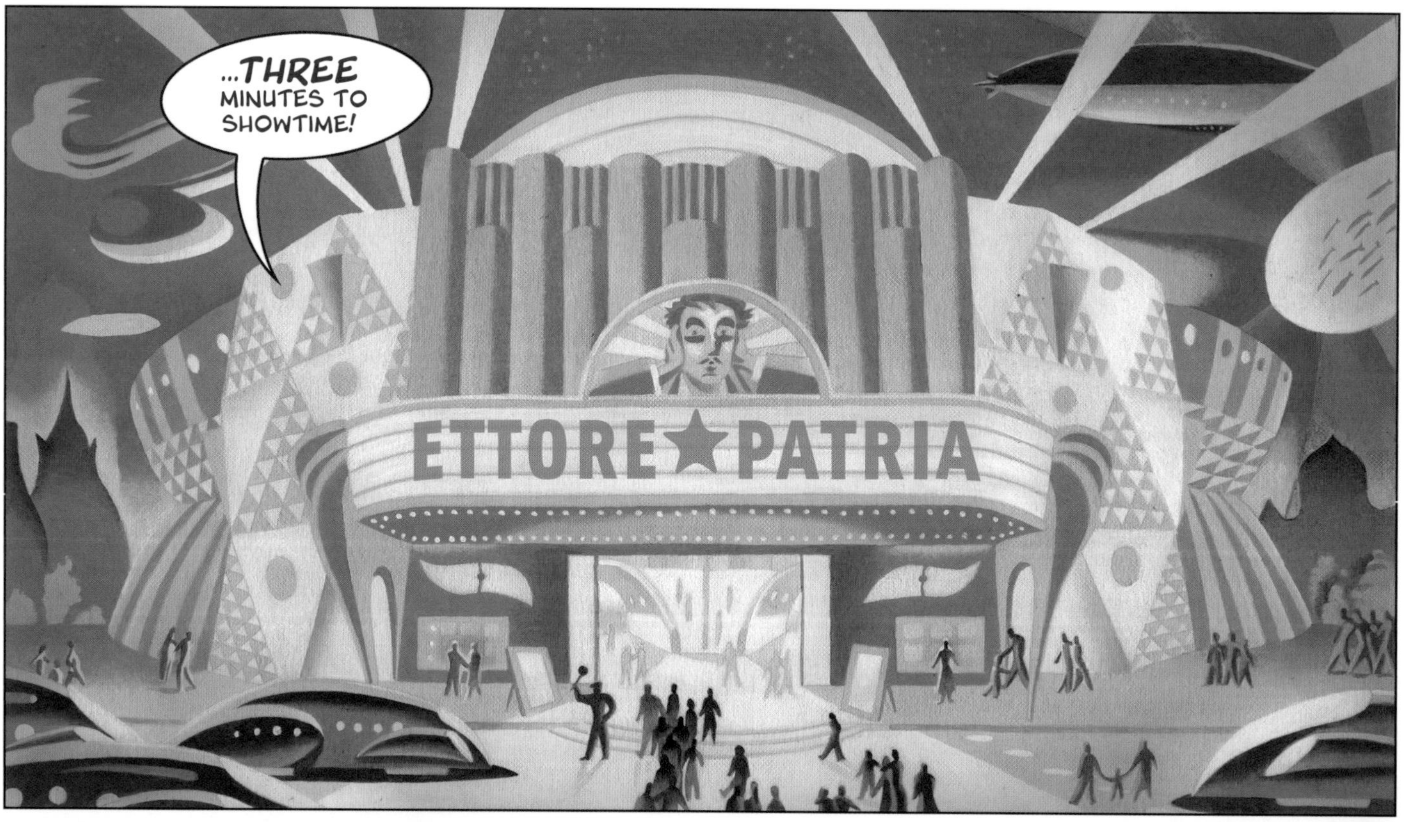
...THREE MINUTES TO SHOWTIME!
ETTORE PATRIA

NOW I JUST HAVE TO CLOSE MY EYES. YESTERDAY IT HAPPENED BEFORE I WENT ON STAGE.

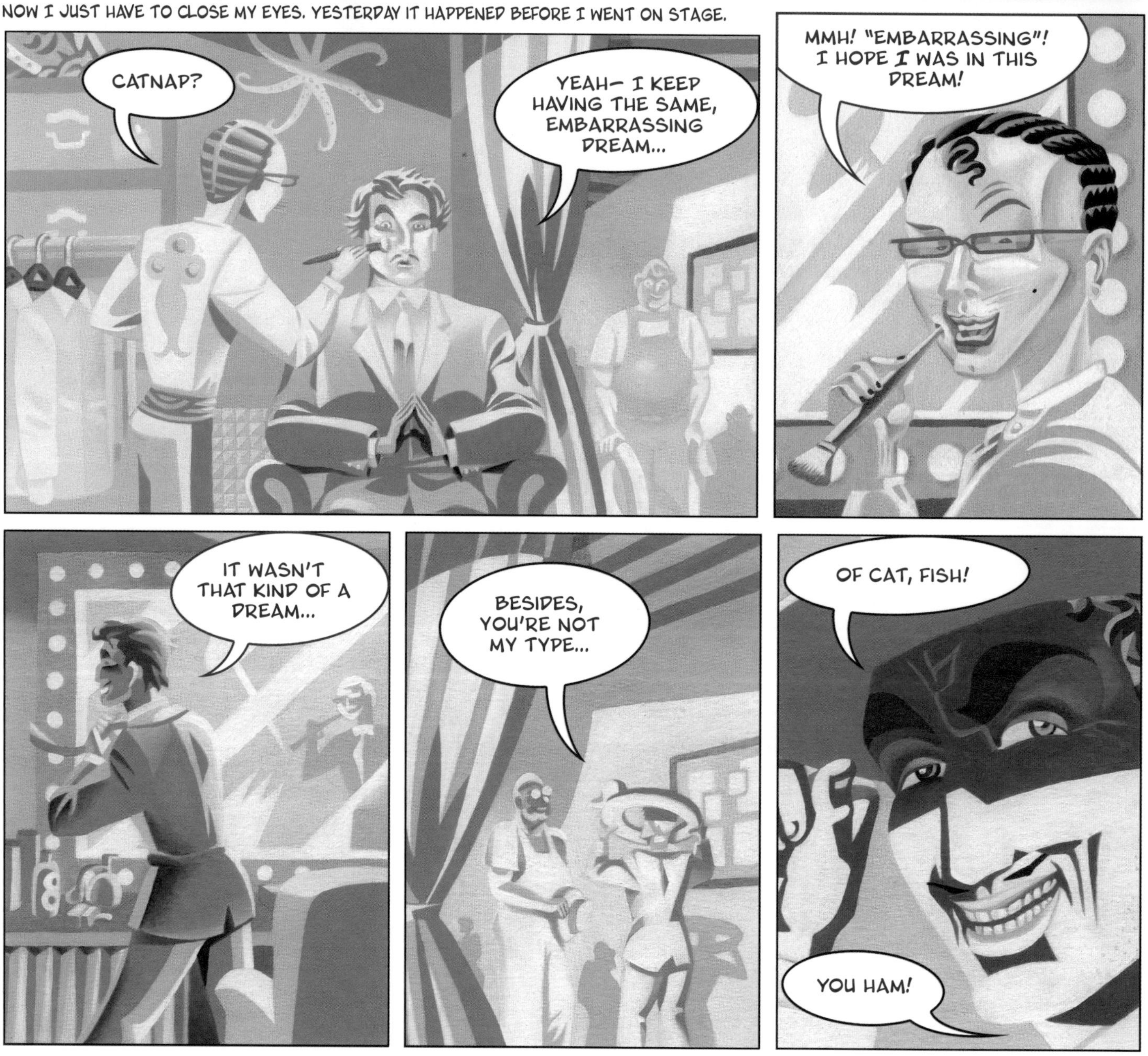
CATNAP?
YEAH— I KEEP HAVING THE SAME, EMBARRASSING DREAM...
MMH! "EMBARRASSING"! I HOPE I WAS IN THIS DREAM!
IT WASN'T THAT KIND OF A DREAM...
BESIDES, YOU'RE NOT MY TYPE...
OF CAT, FISH!
YOU HAM!

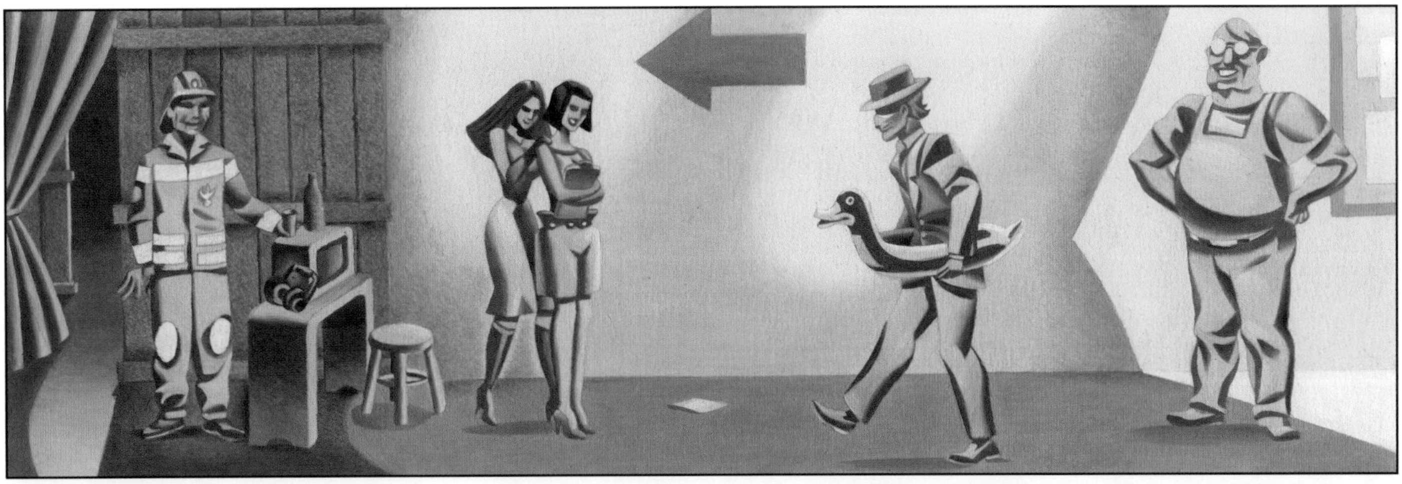

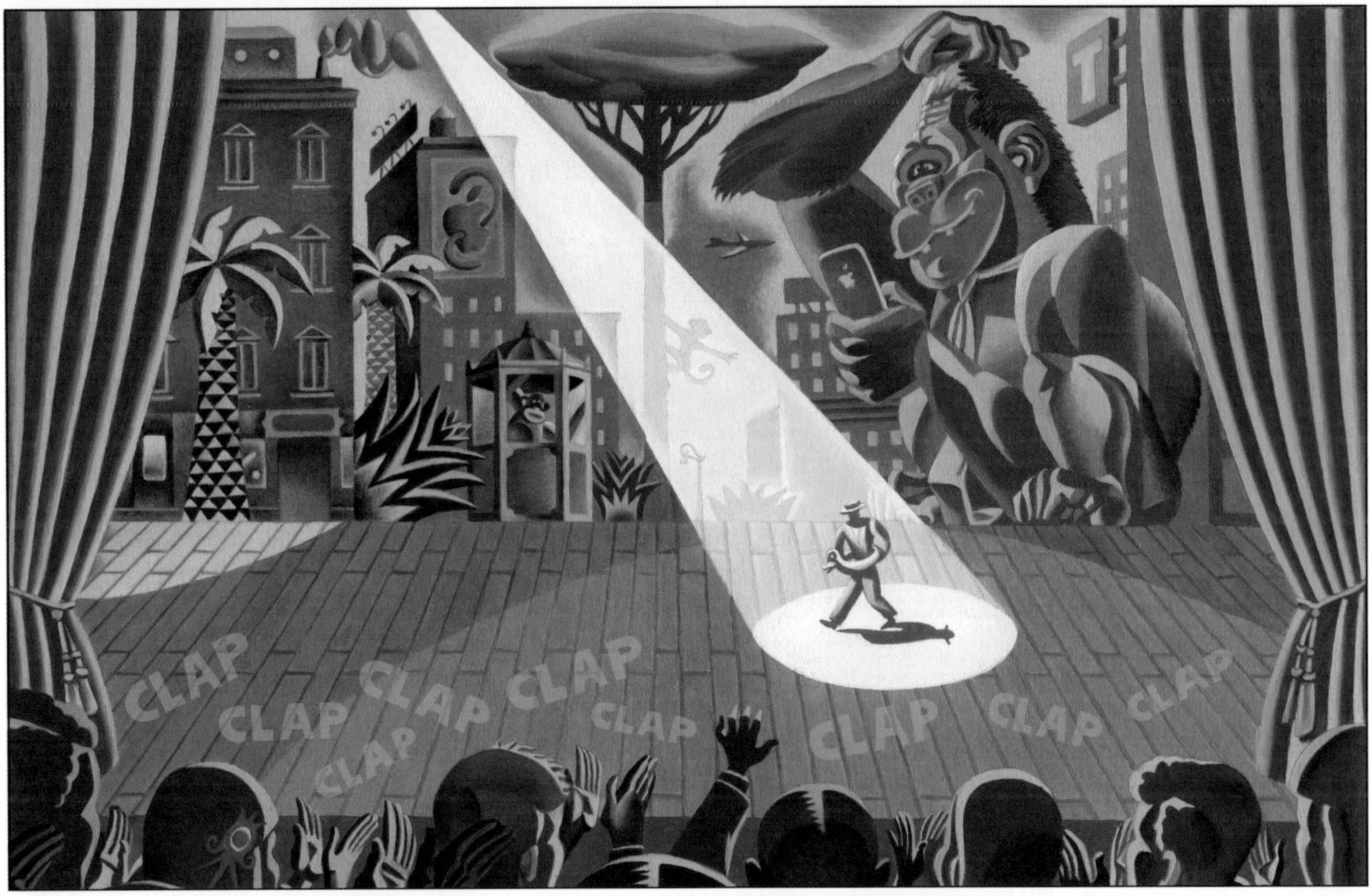
CLAP
CLAP
CLAP
CLAP
CLAP
CLAP
CLAP
CLAP
CLAP
CLAP

"HOW LONG HAVE YOU BEEN PLAYING ETTORE PATRIA?"– "THREE YEARS..."– "JUST LIKE YOUR RHYME: ONE, TWO, THREE..."

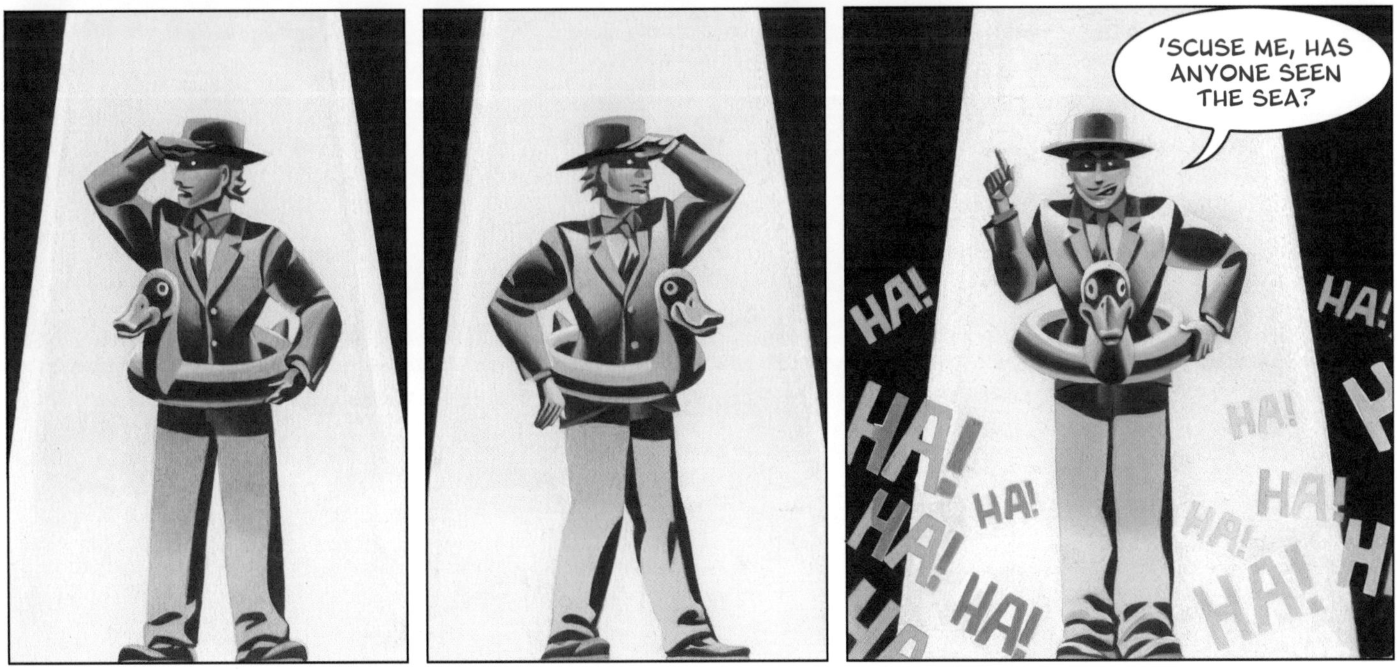
'SCUSE ME, HAS ANYONE SEEN THE SEA?
HA!
HA!
HA!
HA!
HA!
HA!
HA!
HA!
HA!
HA!

"THE AUDIENCE LOVES YOUR 'SURFACE MAN'- BECAUSE HE'S A DUMB, CRASS, EGOTISTICAL CHARACTER WHO CONFIRMS EVERYTHING WE KNOW ABOUT 'THEM'- THAT THEY'RE THE BIGGEST JOKES ON THE PLANET."

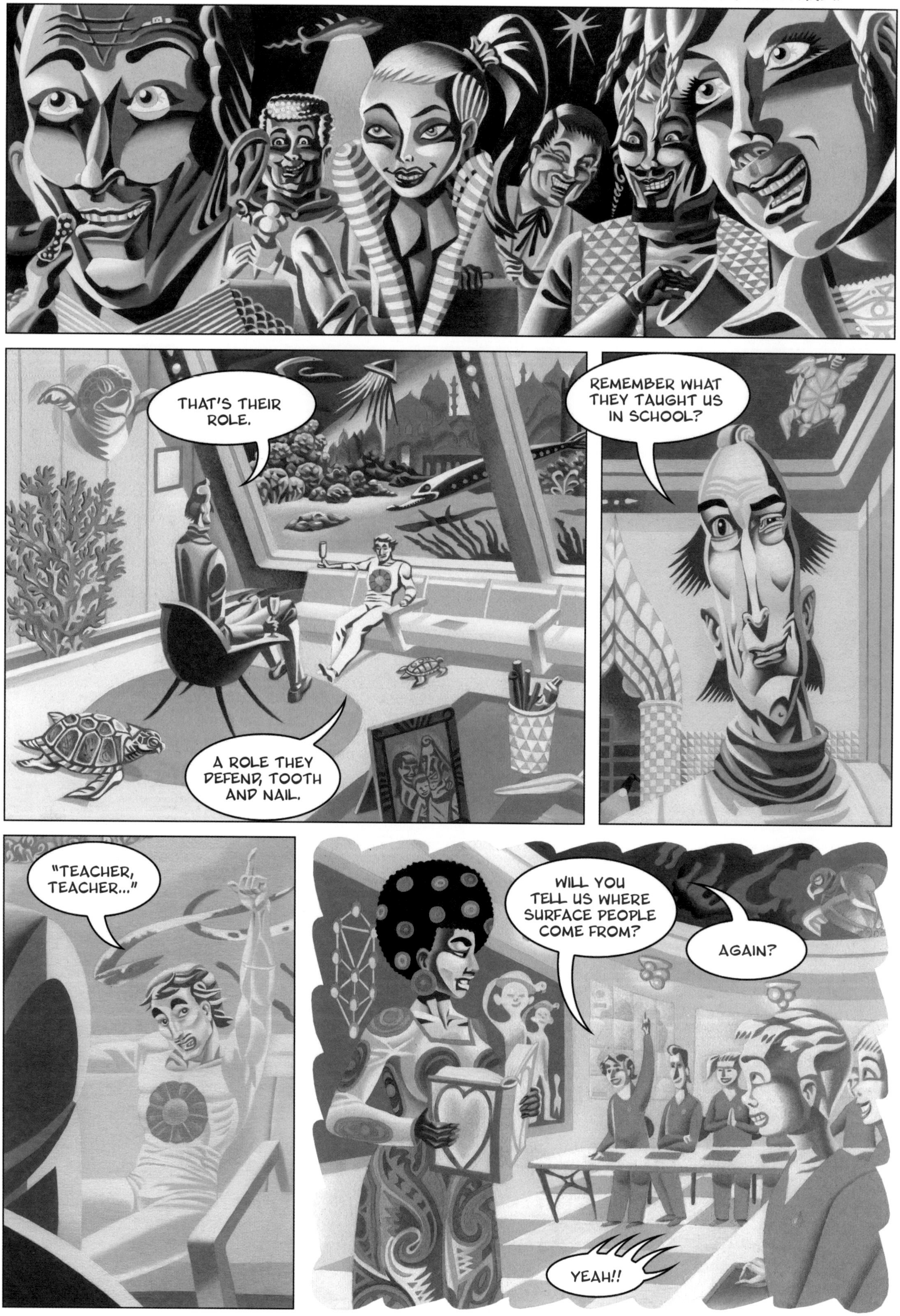
THAT'S THEIR ROLE.
A ROLE THEY DEFEND, TOOTH AND NAIL.
REMEMBER WHAT THEY TAUGHT US IN SCHOOL?
"TEACHER, TEACHER..."
WILL YOU TELL US WHERE SURFACE PEOPLE COME FROM?
AGAIN?
YEAH!!

ONCE UPON A TIME, THERE WAS AN UNHAPPY COUPLE WHO WERE SEARCHING FOR "SOMETHING" BUT COULDN'T FIND IT, PERHAPS BECAUSE THEY DIDN'T KNOW WHAT IT WAS.

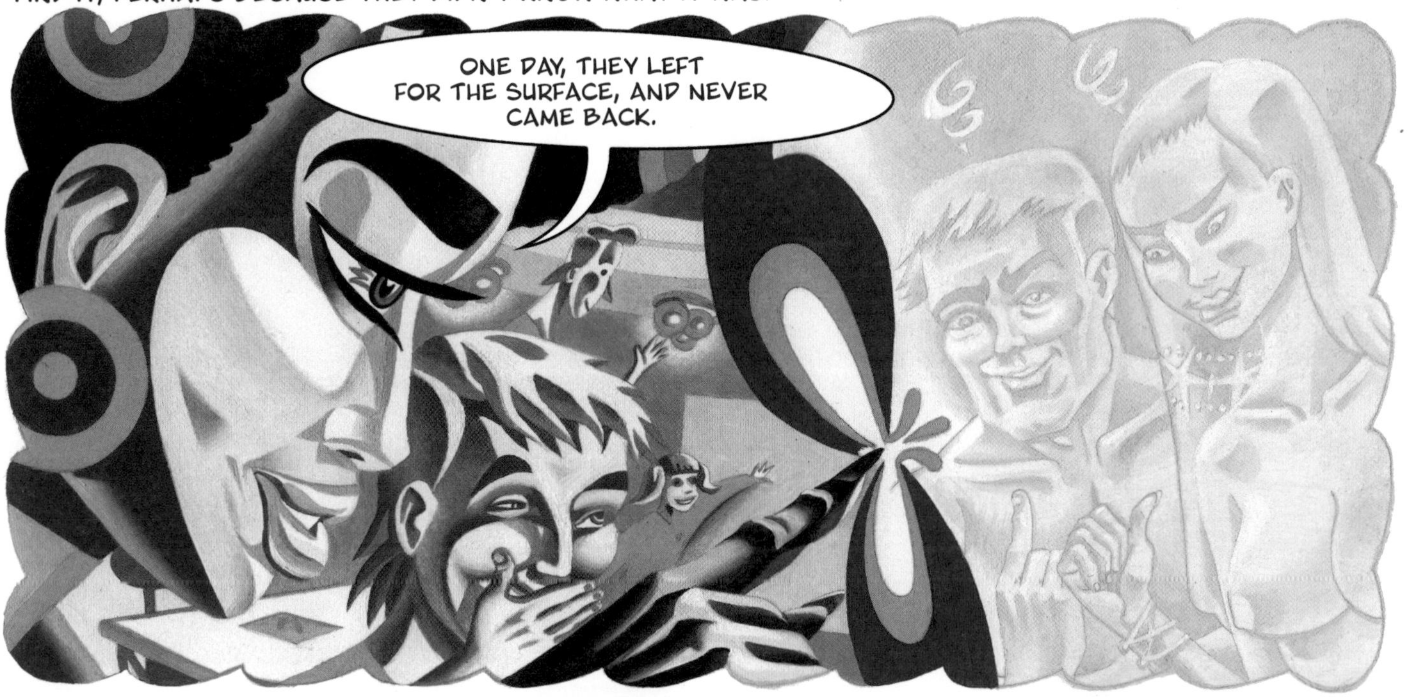
ONE DAY, THEY LEFT FOR THE SURFACE, AND NEVER CAME BACK.

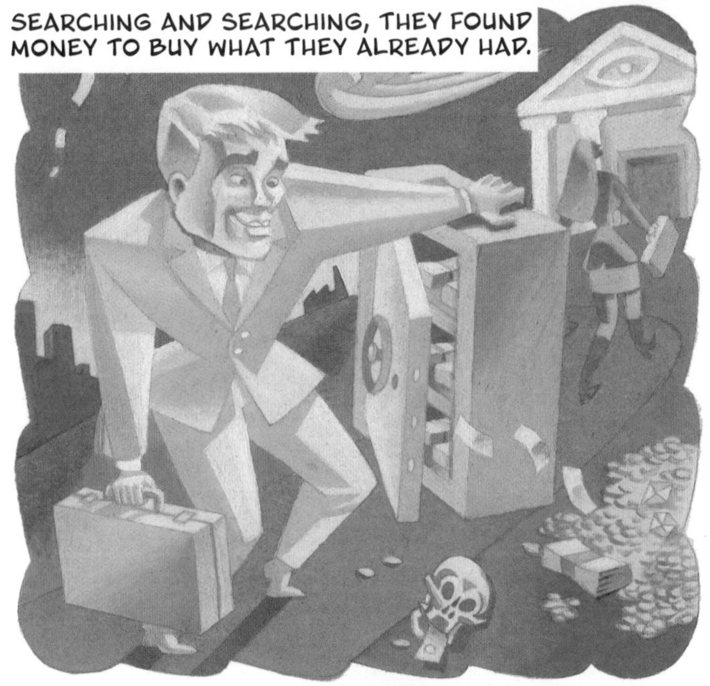
SEARCHING AND SEARCHING, THEY FOUND MONEY TO BUY WHAT THEY ALREADY HAD.

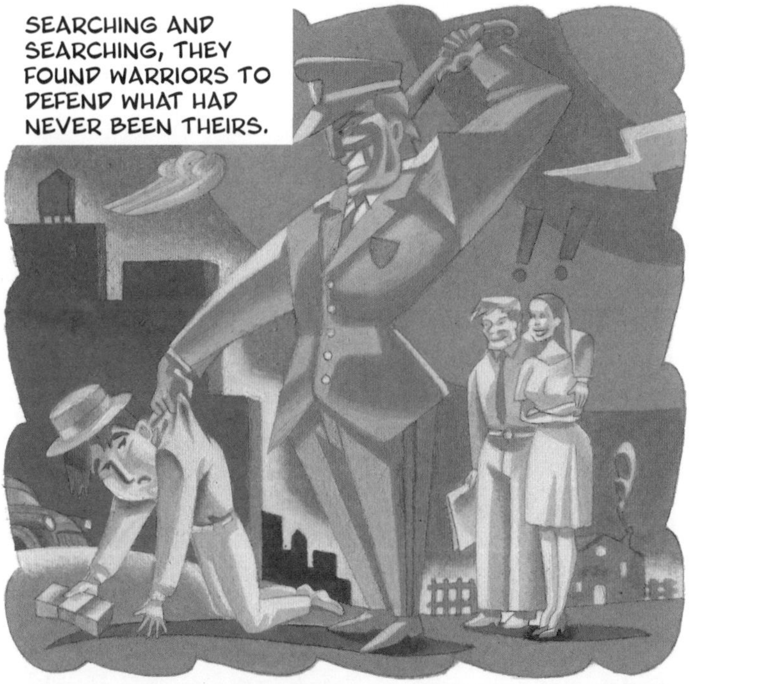
SEARCHING AND SEARCHING, THEY FOUND WARRIORS TO DEFEND WHAT HAD NEVER BEEN THEIRS.

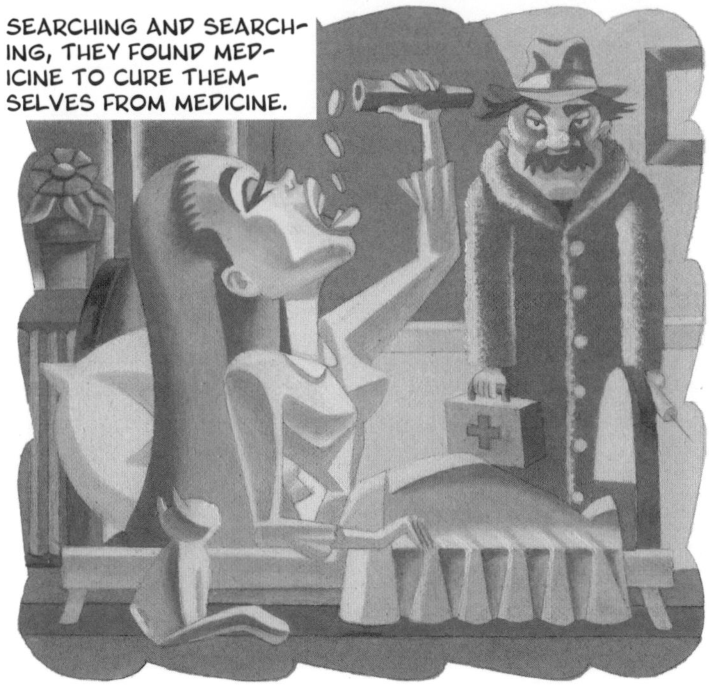
SEARCHING AND SEARCHING, THEY FOUND MEDICINE TO CURE THEMSELVES FROM MEDICINE.

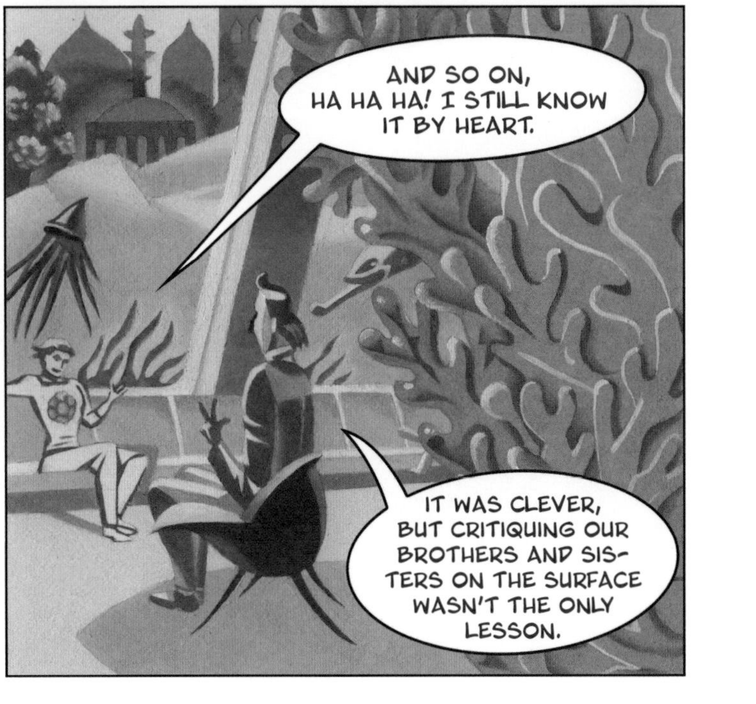
AND SO ON, HA HA HA! I STILL KNOW IT BY HEART.
IT WAS CLEVER, BUT CRITIQUING OUR BROTHERS AND SISTERS ON THE SURFACE WASN'T THE ONLY LESSON.

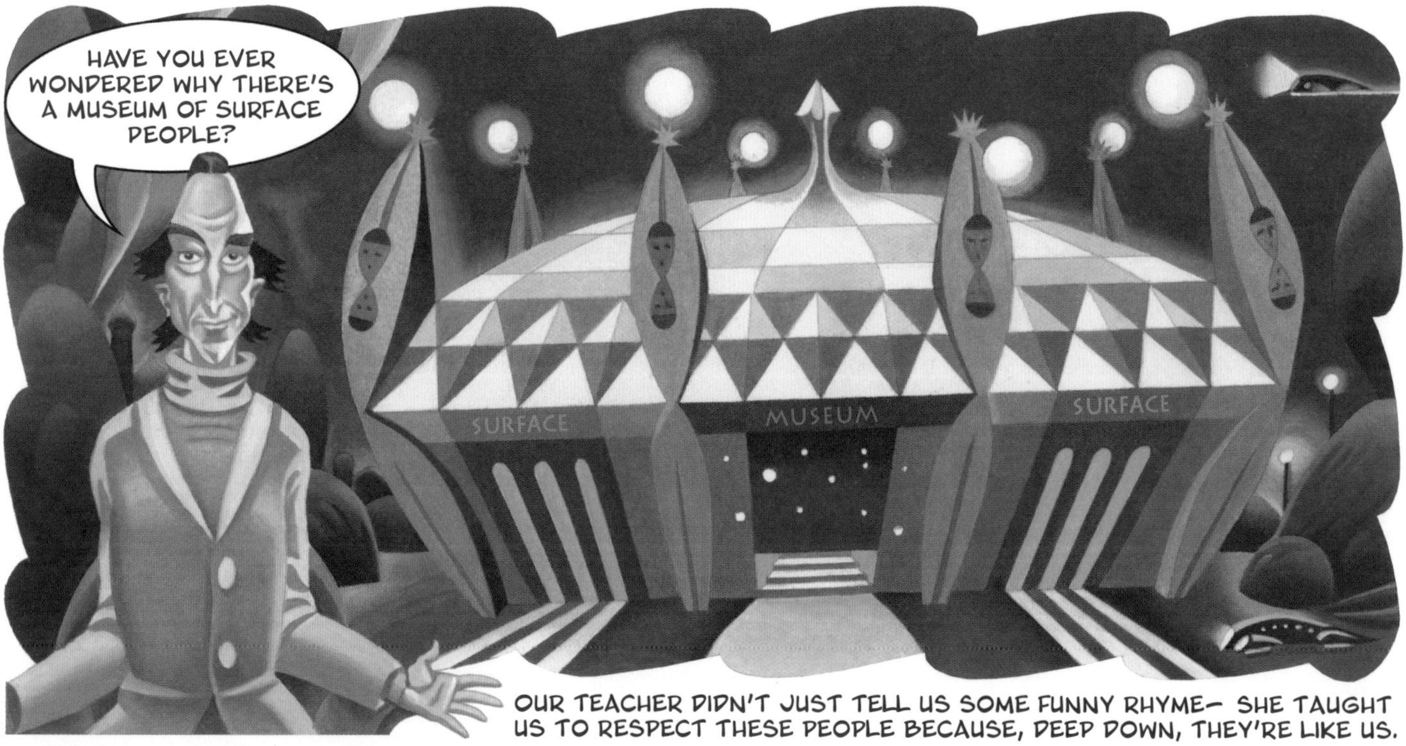
HAVE YOU EVER WONDERED WHY THERE'S A MUSEUM OF SURFACE PEOPLE?
SURFACE
MUSEUM
SURFACE

OUR TEACHER DIDN'T JUST TELL US SOME FUNNY RHYME– SHE TAUGHT US TO RESPECT THESE PEOPLE BECAUSE, DEEP DOWN, THEY'RE LIKE US.

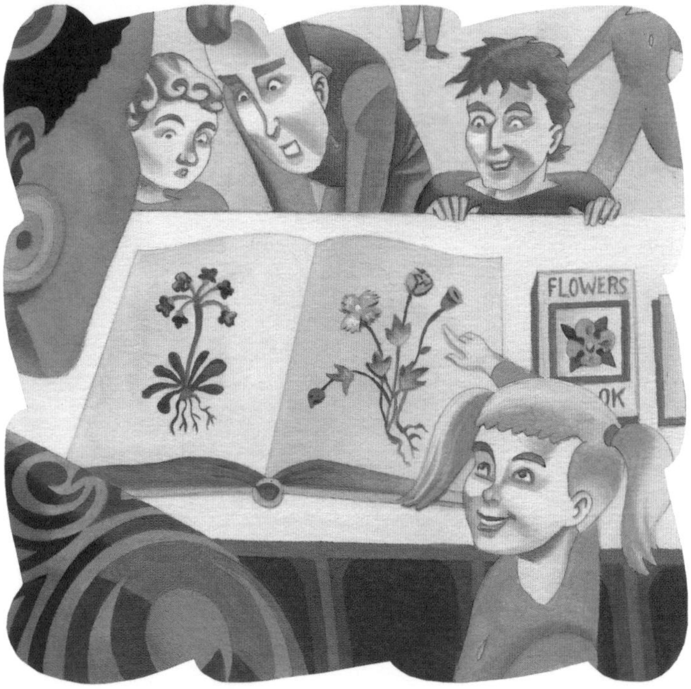
FLOWERS

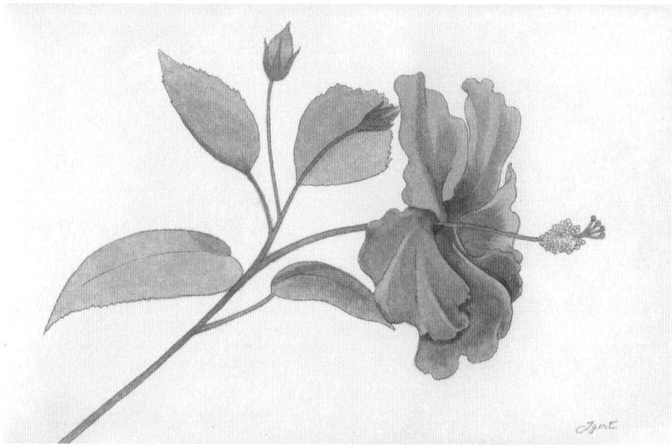

(BY IGORT)

THEY, TOO, LOVE NATURE AND SEEK BEAUTY.

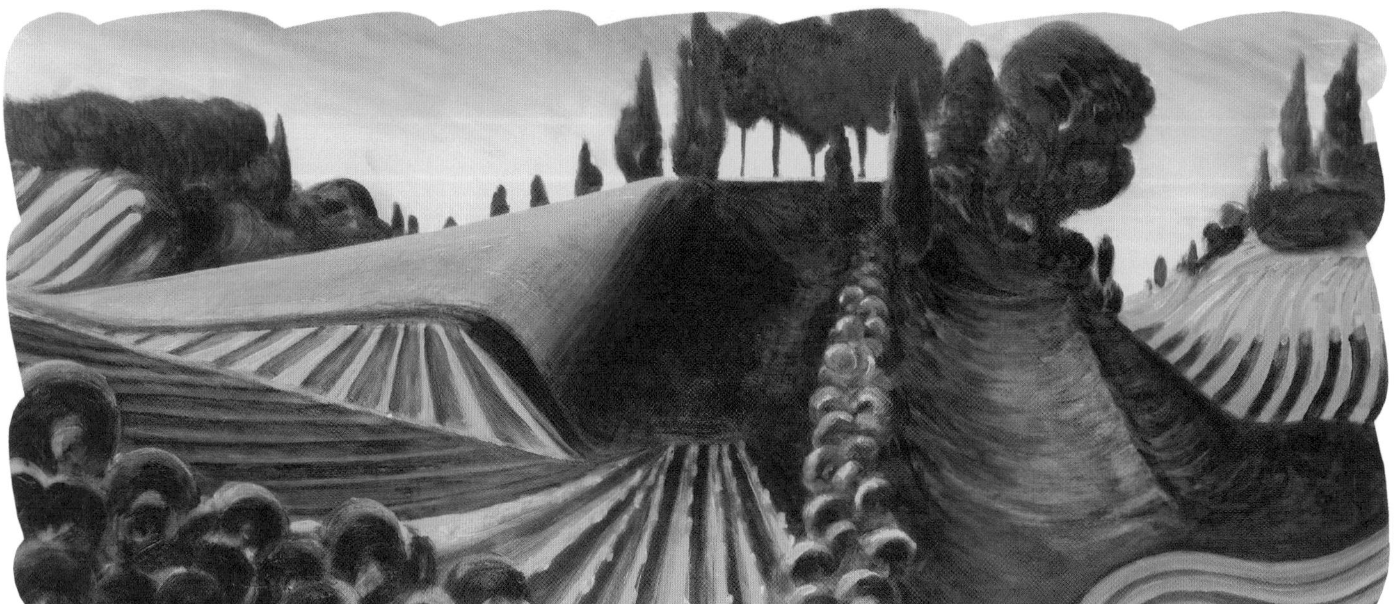

(BY LORENZO MATTOTTI)

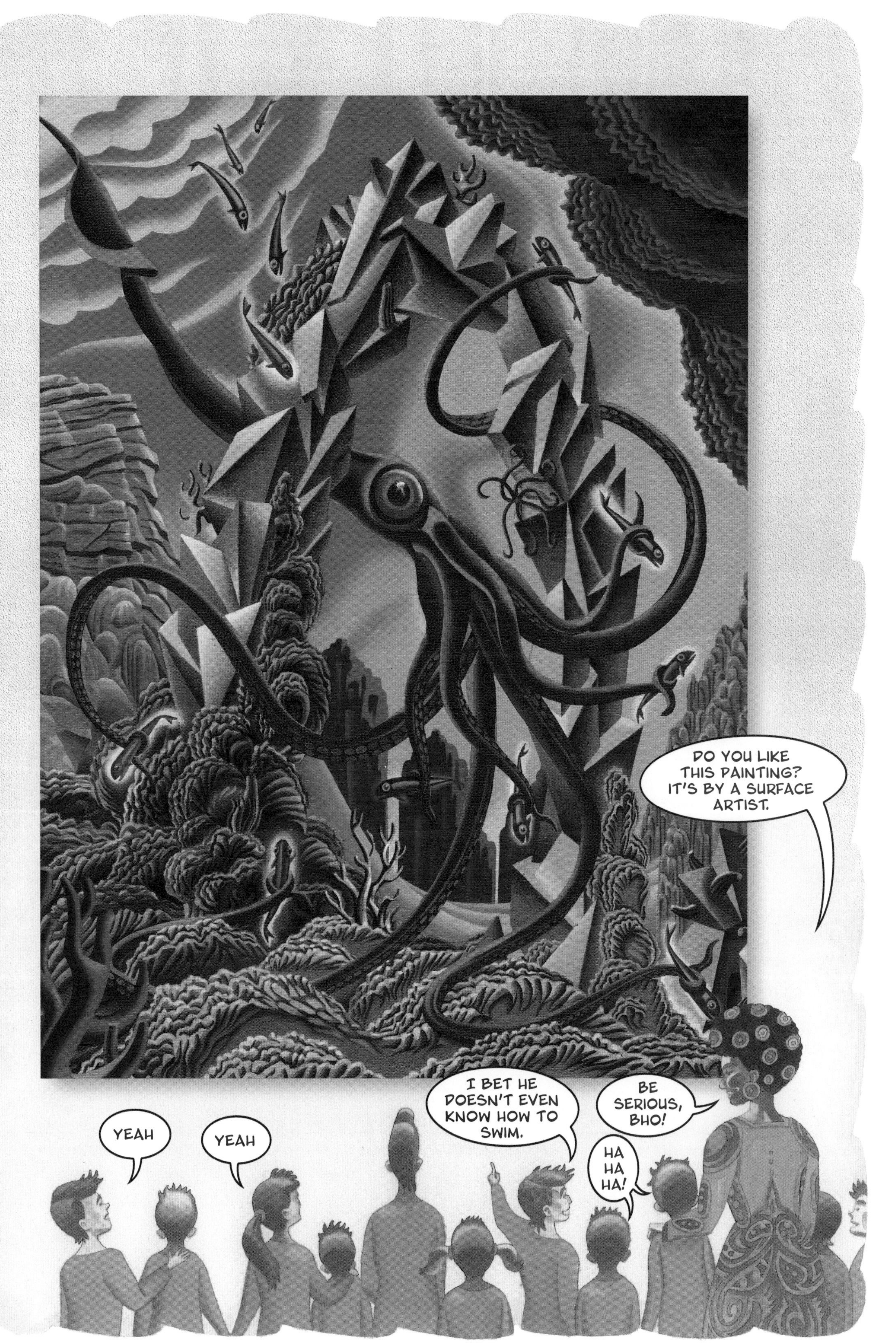
DO YOU LIKE THIS PAINTING? IT'S BY A SURFACE ARTIST.
YEAH
YEAH
I BET HE DOESN'T EVEN KNOW HOW TO SWIM.
BE SERIOUS, BHO!
HA HA HA!

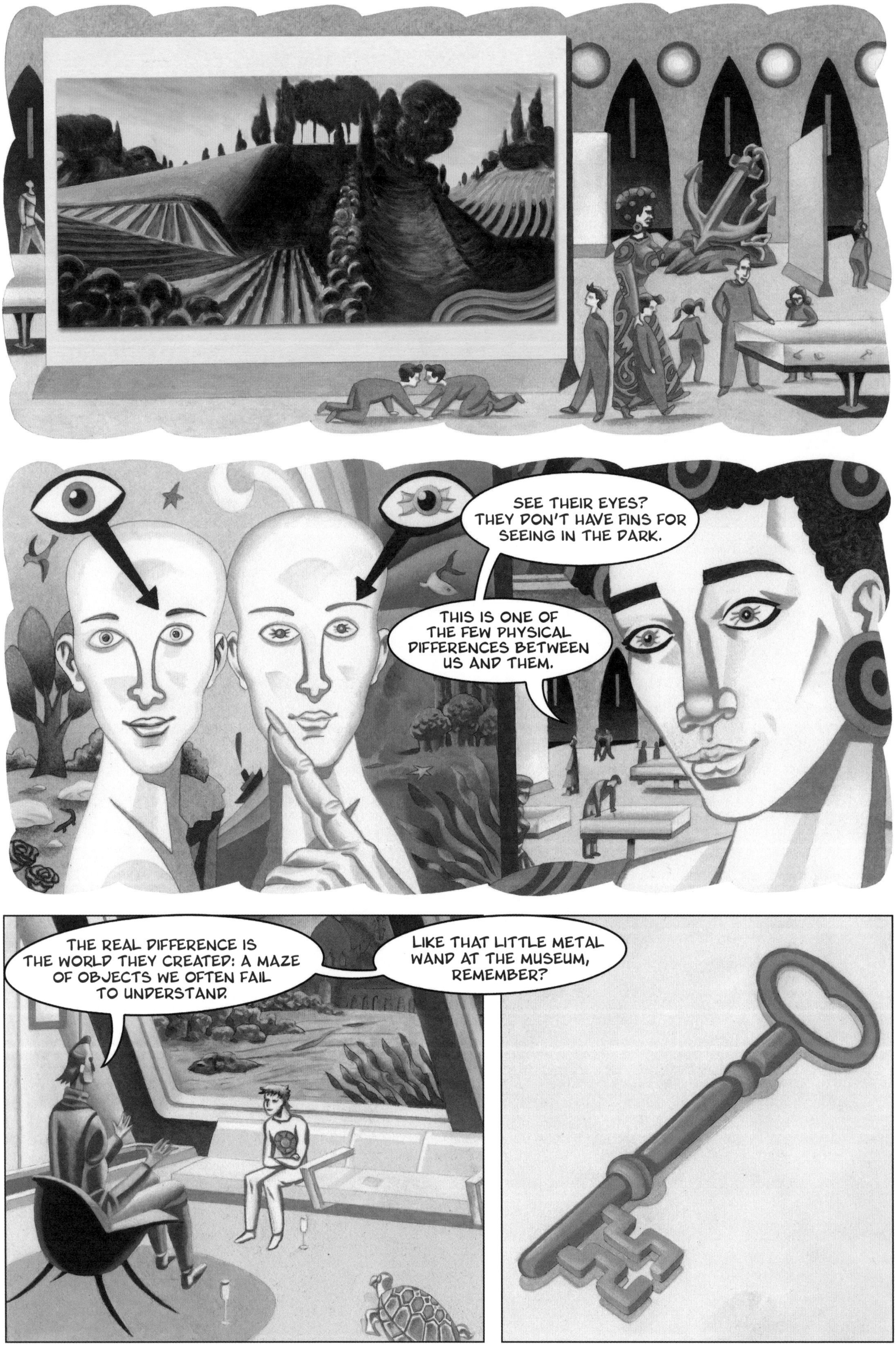
SEE THEIR EYES? THEY DON'T HAVE FINS FOR SEEING IN THE DARK.
THIS IS ONE OF THE FEW PHYSICAL DIFFERENCES BETWEEN US AND THEM.
THE REAL DIFFERENCE IS THE WORLD THEY CREATED: A MAZE OF OBJECTS WE OFTEN FAIL TO UNDERSTAND.
LIKE THAT LITTLE METAL WAND AT THE MUSEUM, REMEMBER?

THAT THING WITH A SORT OF HANDLE?

NO, THAT'S IN THE SAME ROOM, BUT THAT'S NOT THE POINT...

WHAT I'M TRYING TO TELL YOU IS THAT ALTHOUGH THERE ARE NO TWO CIVILIZATIONS MORE DISTANT...

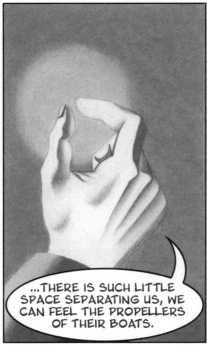

...THERE IS SUCH LITTLE SPACE SEPARATING US, WE CAN FEEL THE PROPELLERS OF THEIR BOATS.

WE'RE BOUND BY A COMMON FATE.

BUT WOE IF OUR COMMUNITIES WERE TO COME INTO CONTACT!

IT'D BE THE END OF BOTH!

OUR DAILY SONG PROTECTS THEM AS WELL...

HOWEVER, IT'S THE ONE FRAGILE THING HOLDING BACK THE CHAOS.

BUT... BACK TO US...

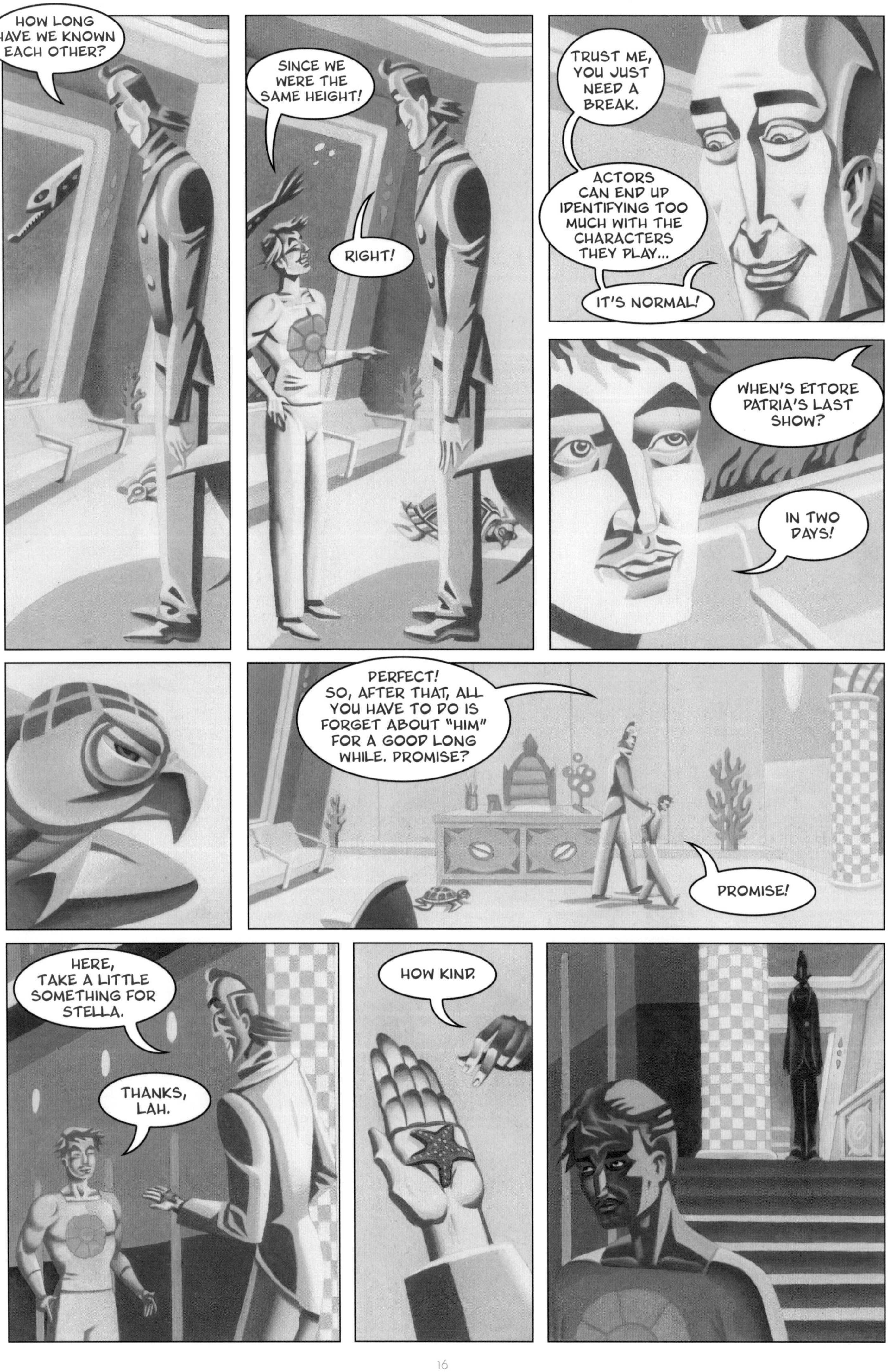
HOW LONG HAVE WE KNOWN EACH OTHER?
SINCE WE WERE THE SAME HEIGHT!
RIGHT!
TRUST ME, YOU JUST NEED A BREAK.
ACTORS CAN END UP IDENTIFYING TOO MUCH WITH THE CHARACTERS THEY PLAY...
IT'S NORMAL!
WHEN'S ETTORE PATRIA'S LAST SHOW?
IN TWO DAYS!
PERFECT! SO, AFTER THAT, ALL YOU HAVE TO DO IS FORGET ABOUT "HIM" FOR A GOOD LONG WHILE. PROMISE?
PROMISE!
HERE, TAKE A LITTLE SOMETHING FOR STELLA.
THANKS, LAH.
HOW KIND.

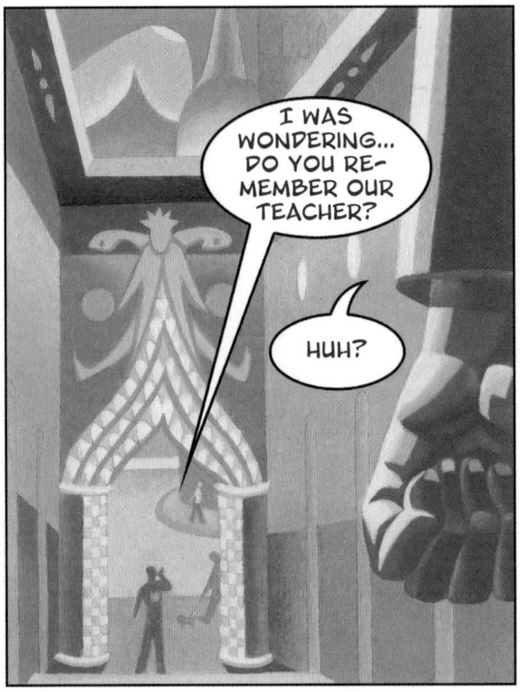
I WAS WONDERING... DO YOU RE- MEMBER OUR TEACHER?
HUH?
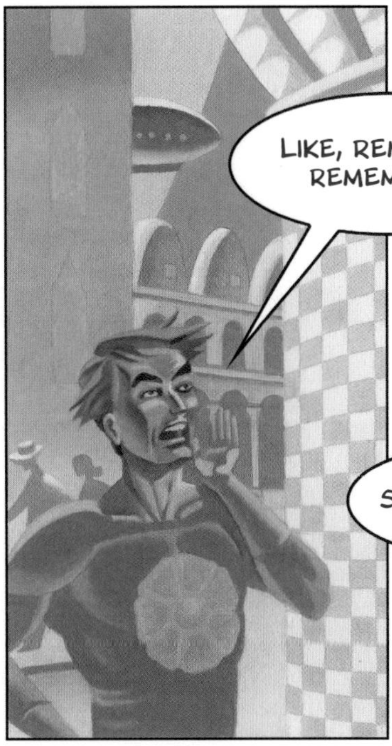
LIKE, REMEMBER REMEMBER?
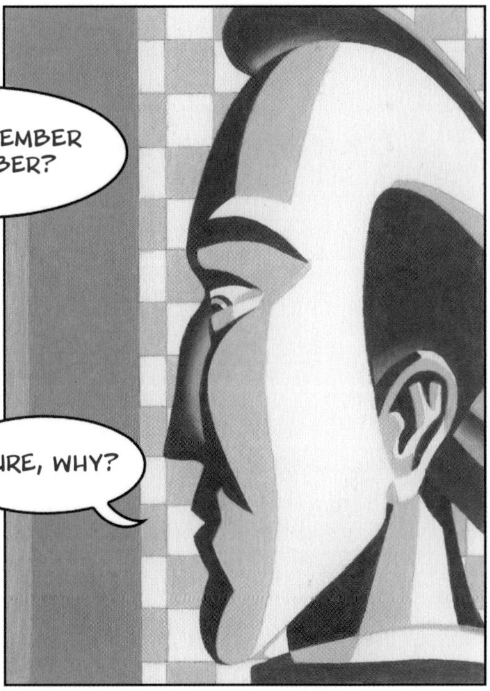
SURE, WHY?
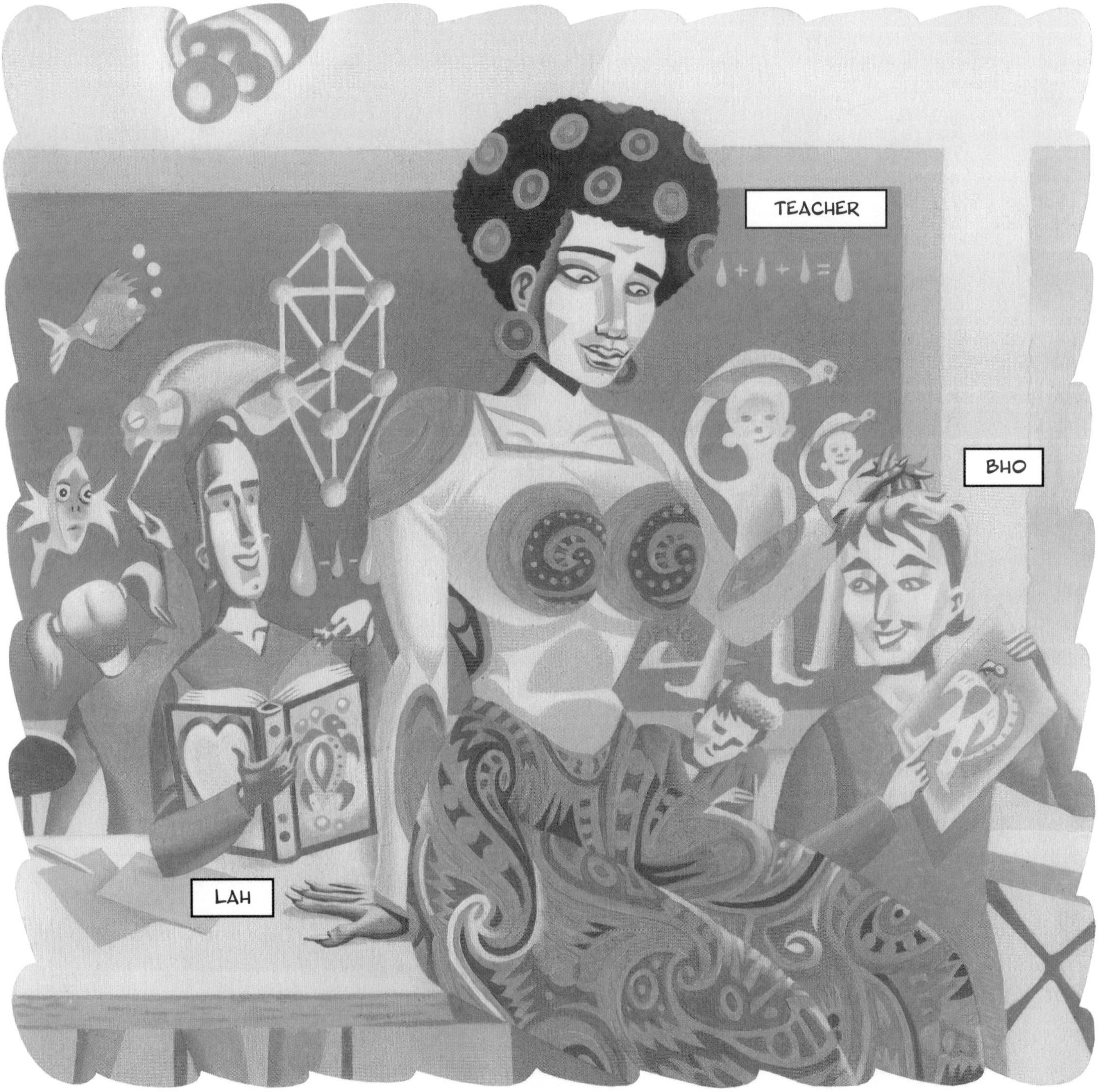
TEACHER
BHO
LAH

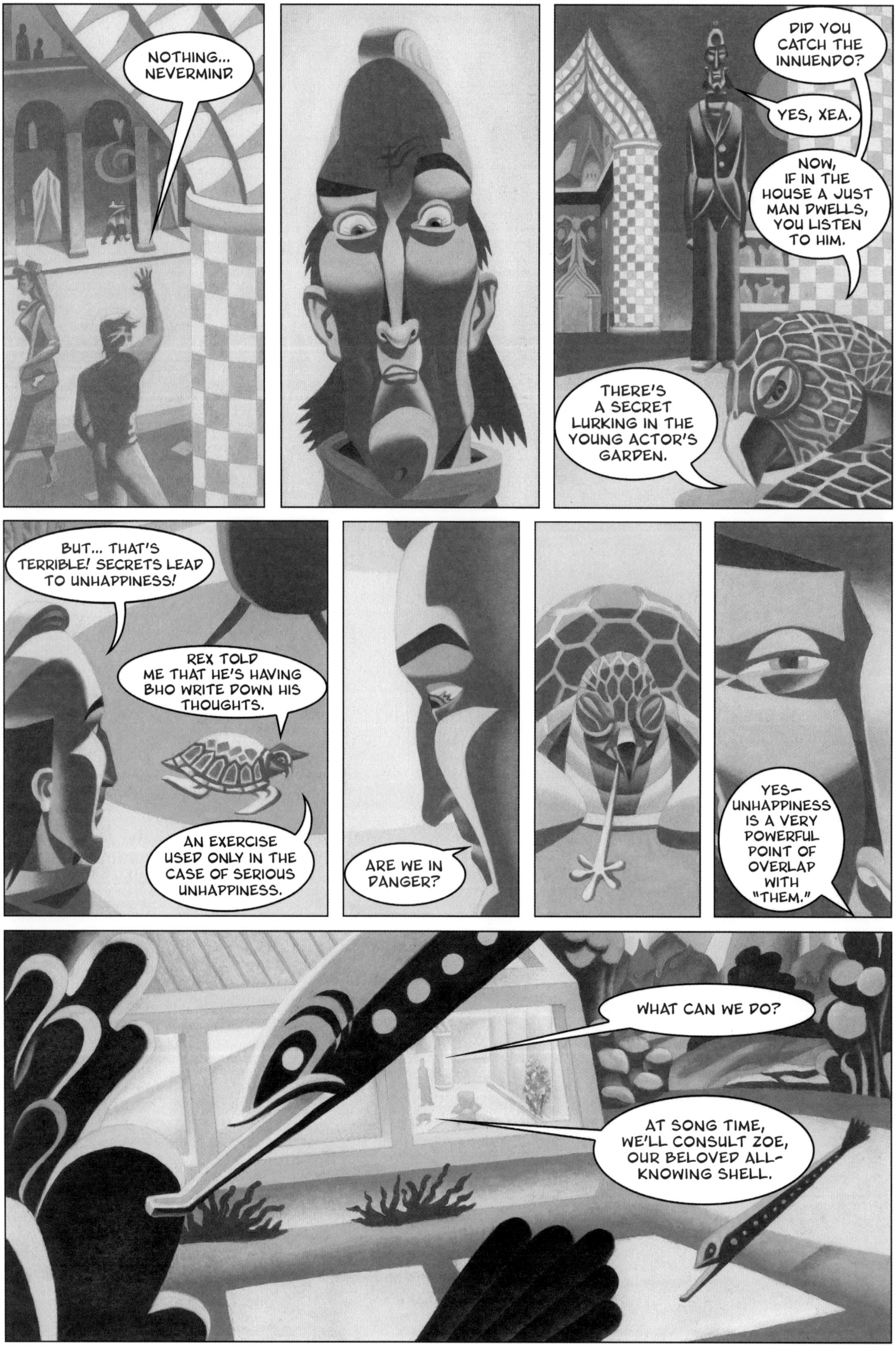
NOTHING... NEVERMIND.
DID YOU CATCH THE INNUENDO?
YES, XEA.
NOW, IF IN THE HOUSE A JUST MAN DWELLS, YOU LISTEN TO HIM.
THERE'S A SECRET LURKING IN THE YOUNG ACTOR'S GARDEN.
BUT... THAT'S TERRIBLE! SECRETS LEAD TO UNHAPPINESS!
REX TOLD ME THAT HE'S HAVING BHO WRITE DOWN HIS THOUGHTS.
AN EXERCISE USED ONLY IN THE CASE OF SERIOUS UNHAPPINESS.
ARE WE IN DANGER?
YES— UNHAPPINESS IS A VERY POWERFUL POINT OF OVERLAP WITH "THEM."
WHAT CAN WE DO?
AT SONG TIME, WE'LL CONSULT ZOE, OUR BELOVED ALL-KNOWING SHELL.

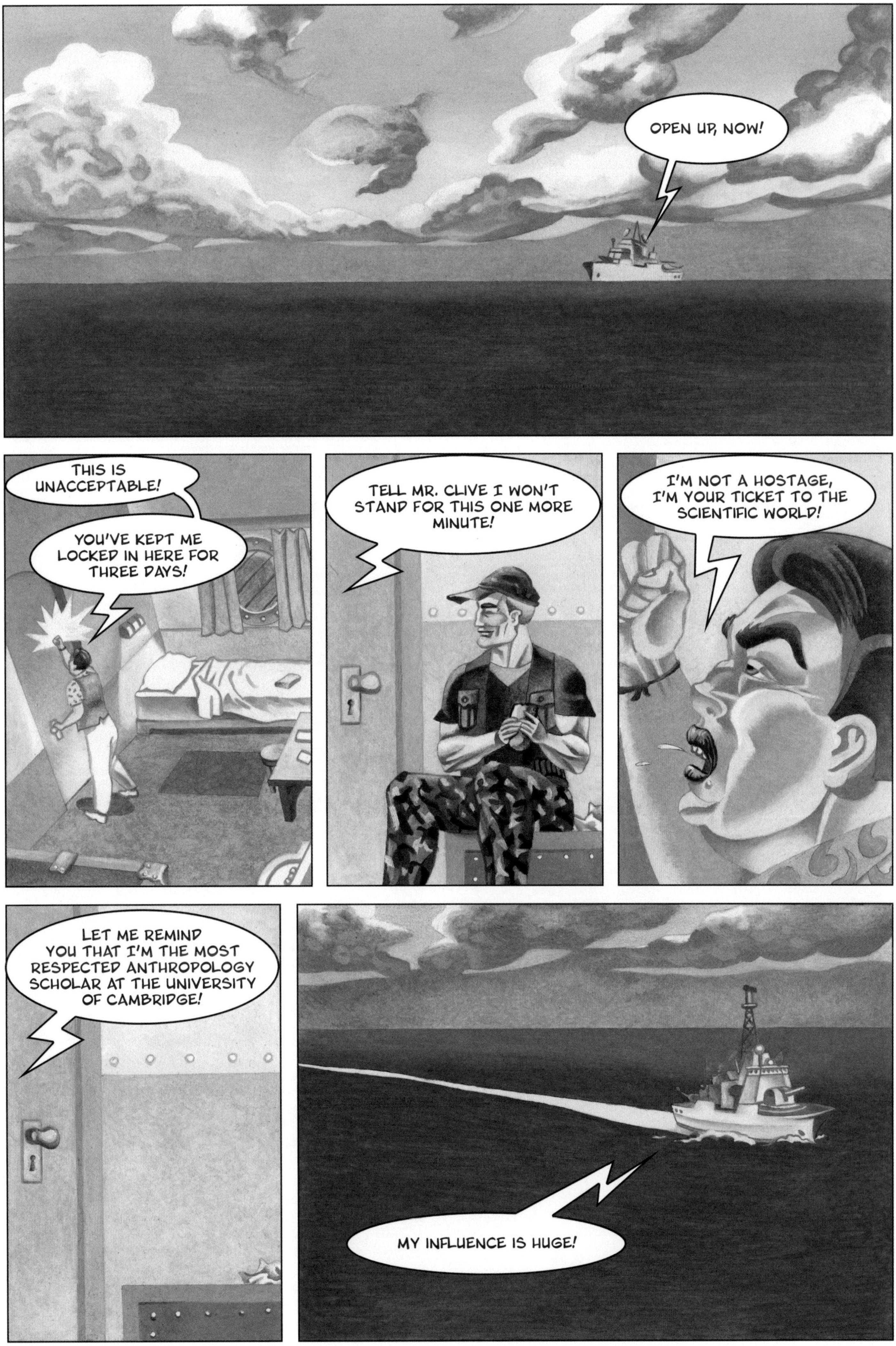
OPEN UP, NOW!
THIS IS UNACCEPTABLE!
YOU'VE KEPT ME LOCKED IN HERE FOR THREE DAYS!
TELL MR. CLIVE I WON'T STAND FOR THIS ONE MORE MINUTE!
I'M NOT A HOSTAGE, I'M YOUR TICKET TO THE SCIENTIFIC WORLD!
LET ME REMIND YOU THAT I'M THE MOST RESPECTED ANTHROPOLOGY SCHOLAR AT THE UNIVERSITY OF CAMBRIDGE!
MY INFLUENCE IS HUGE!

Dear Rex, I've lost control of my character. Ettore Patria is starting to take over.

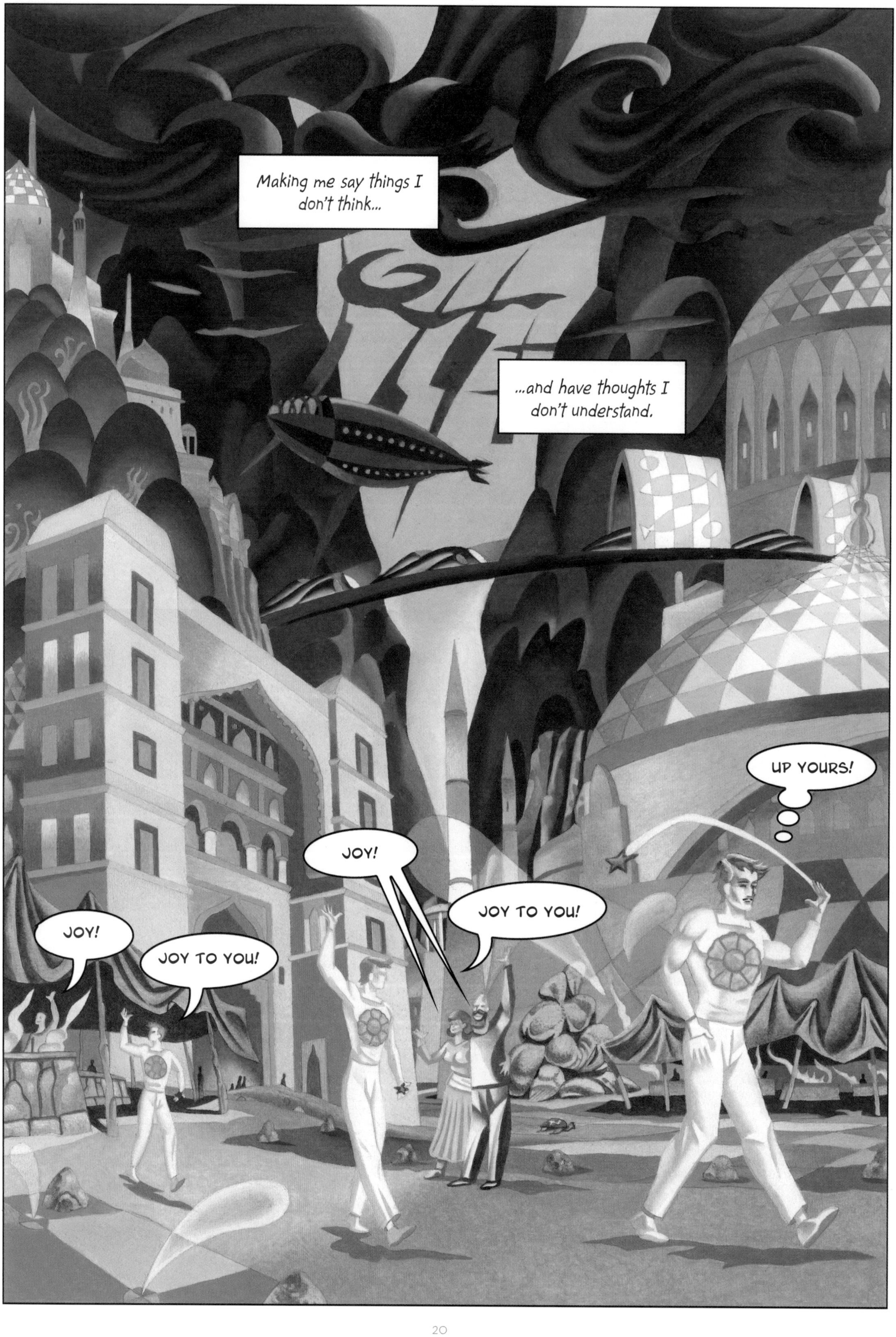
Making me say things I don't think...
...and have thoughts I don't understand.
UP YOURS!
JOY!
JOY TO YOU!
JOY!
JOY TO YOU!

On my way home, I paused at the Surface Museum. I turned and went in.
SURFACE
Walking helps clear my mind of certain nagging thoughts.
WHAT ARE YOU?
WHAT ARE YOU?

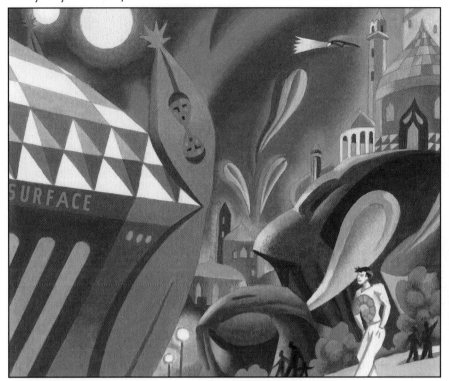

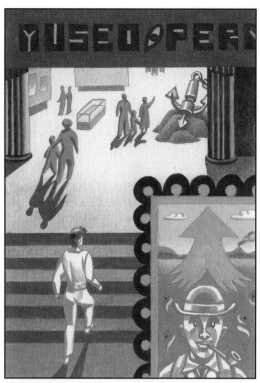

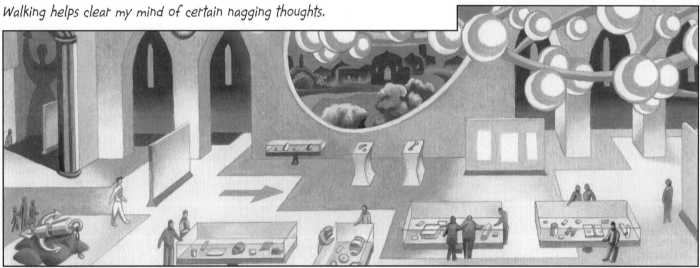

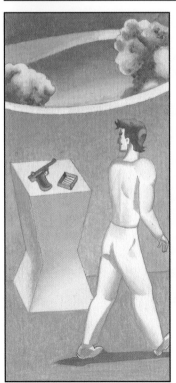

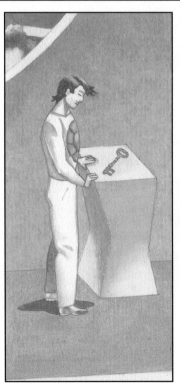

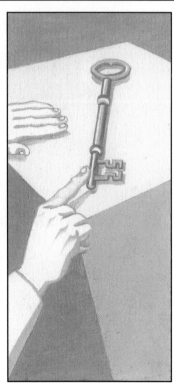

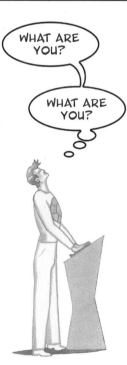

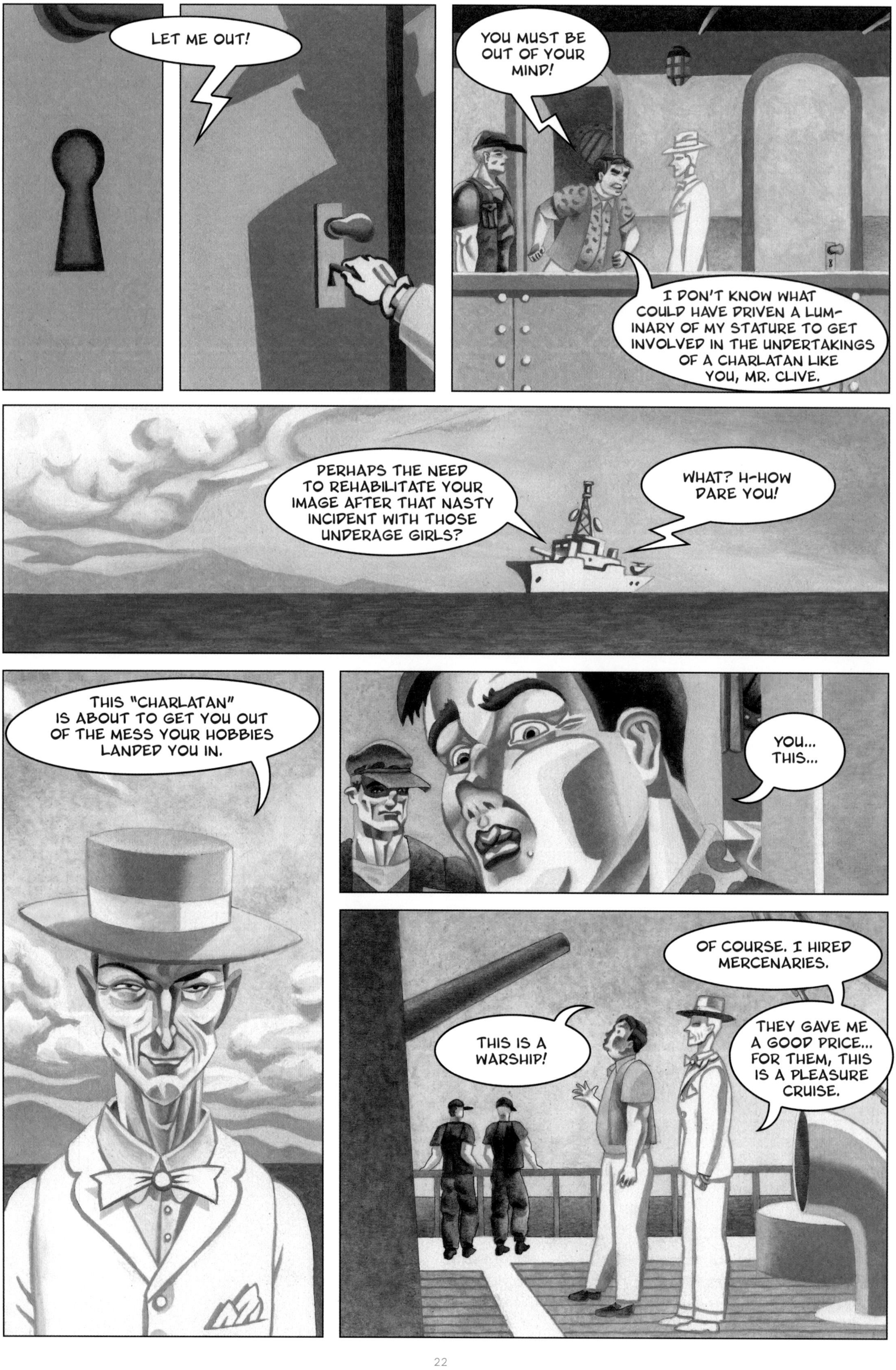
LET ME OUT!
YOU MUST BE OUT OF YOUR MIND!
I DON'T KNOW WHAT COULD HAVE DRIVEN A LUMINARY OF MY STATURE TO GET INVOLVED IN THE UNDERTAKINGS OF A CHARLATAN LIKE YOU, MR. CLIVE.
PERHAPS THE NEED TO REHABILITATE YOUR IMAGE AFTER THAT NASTY INCIDENT WITH THOSE UNDERAGE GIRLS?
WHAT? H-HOW DARE YOU!
THIS "CHARLATAN" IS ABOUT TO GET YOU OUT OF THE MESS YOUR HOBBIES LANDED YOU IN.
YOU... THIS...
OF COURSE. I HIRED MERCENARIES.
THIS IS A WARSHIP!
THEY GAVE ME A GOOD PRICE... FOR THEM, THIS IS A PLEASURE CRUISE.

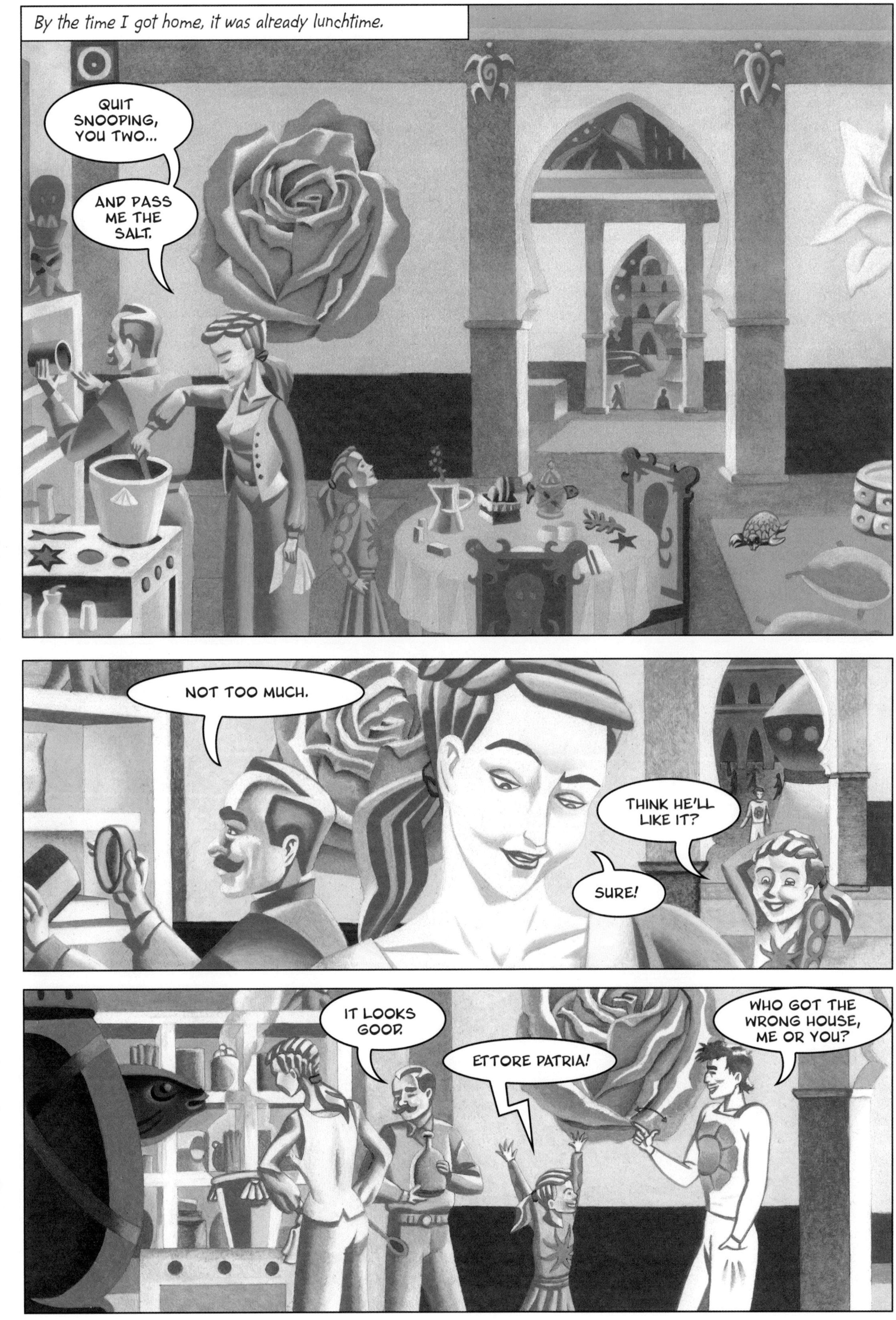

By the time I got home, it was already lunchtime.
QUIT SNOOPING, YOU TWO...
AND PASS ME THE SALT.
NOT TOO MUCH.
THINK HE'LL LIKE IT?
SURE!
IT LOOKS GOOD.
ETTORE PATRIA!
WHO GOT THE WRONG HOUSE, ME OR YOU?

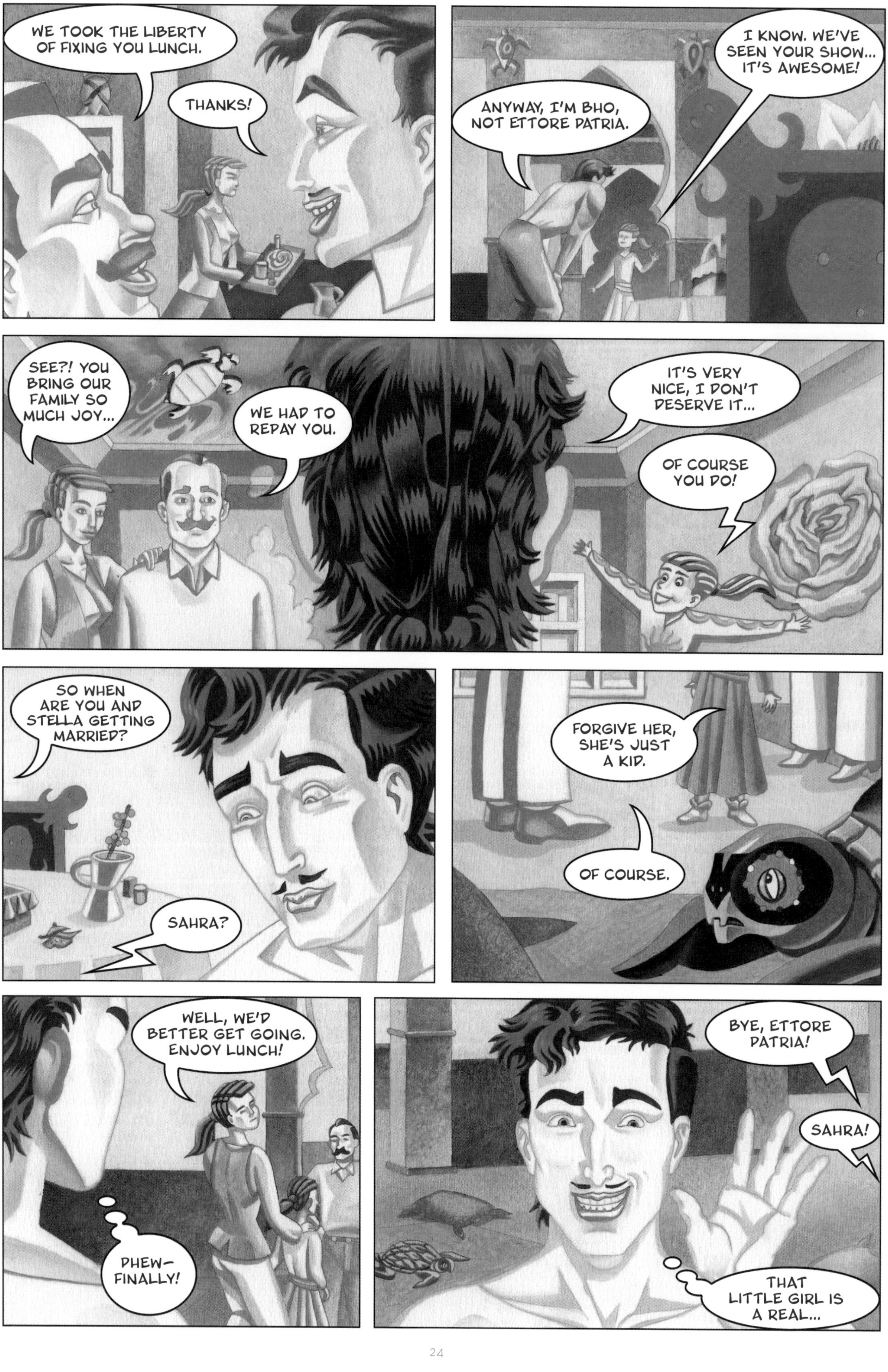
WE TOOK THE LIBERTY OF FIXING YOU LUNCH.
THANKS!
ANYWAY, I'M BHO, NOT ETTORE PATRIA.
I KNOW. WE'VE SEEN YOUR SHOW... IT'S AWESOME!
SEE?! YOU BRING OUR FAMILY SO MUCH JOY...
WE HAD TO REPAY YOU.
IT'S VERY NICE, I DON'T DESERVE IT...
OF COURSE YOU DO!
SO WHEN ARE YOU AND STELLA GETTING MARRIED?
SAHRA?
FORGIVE HER, SHE'S JUST A KID.
OF COURSE.
WELL, WE'D BETTER GET GOING. ENJOY LUNCH!
PHEW— FINALLY!
BYE, ETTORE PATRIA!
SAHRA!
THAT LITTLE GIRL IS A REAL...

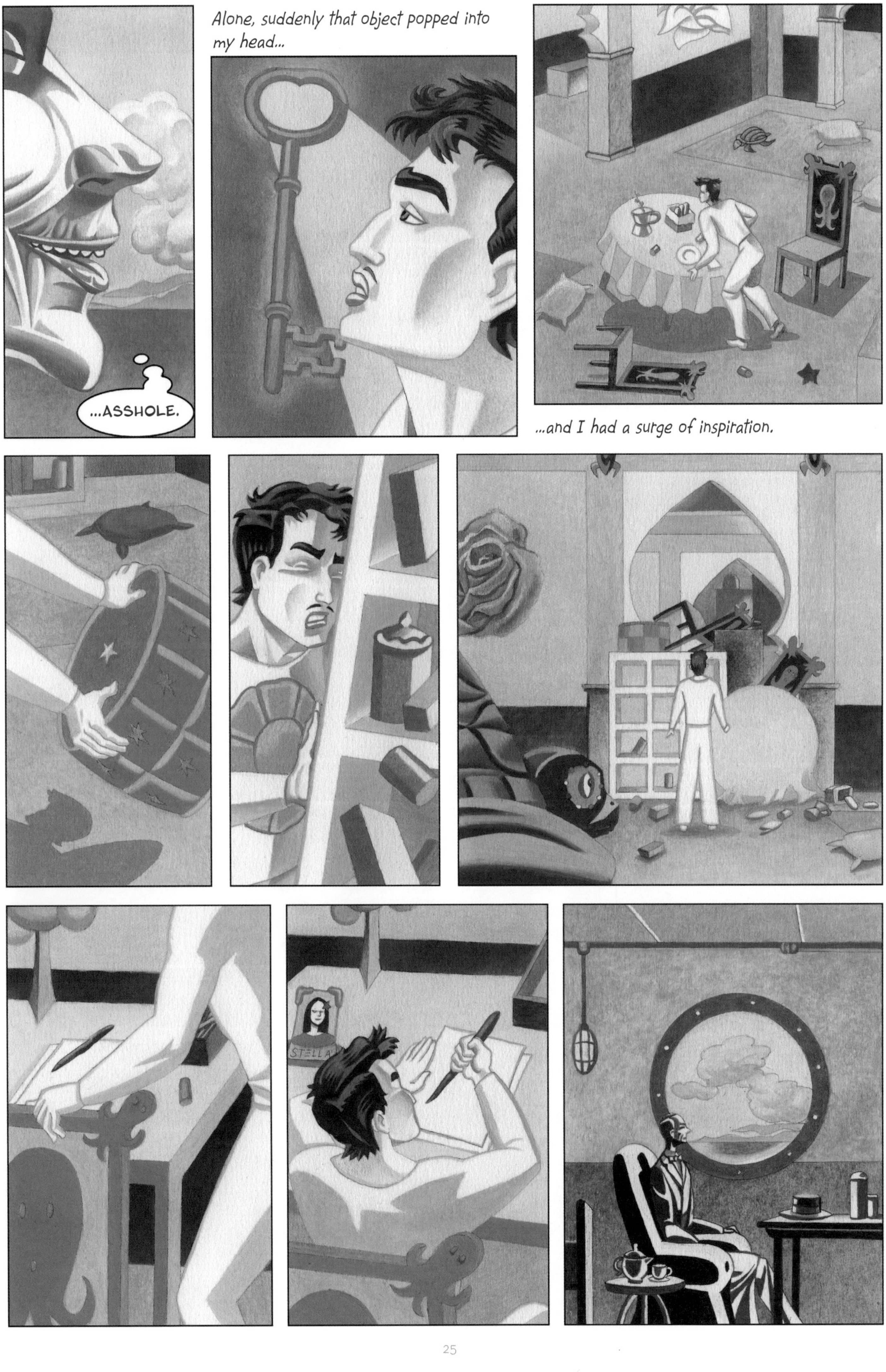
...ASSHOLE.
Alone, suddenly that object popped into my head...
...and I had a surge of inspiration.
STELLA

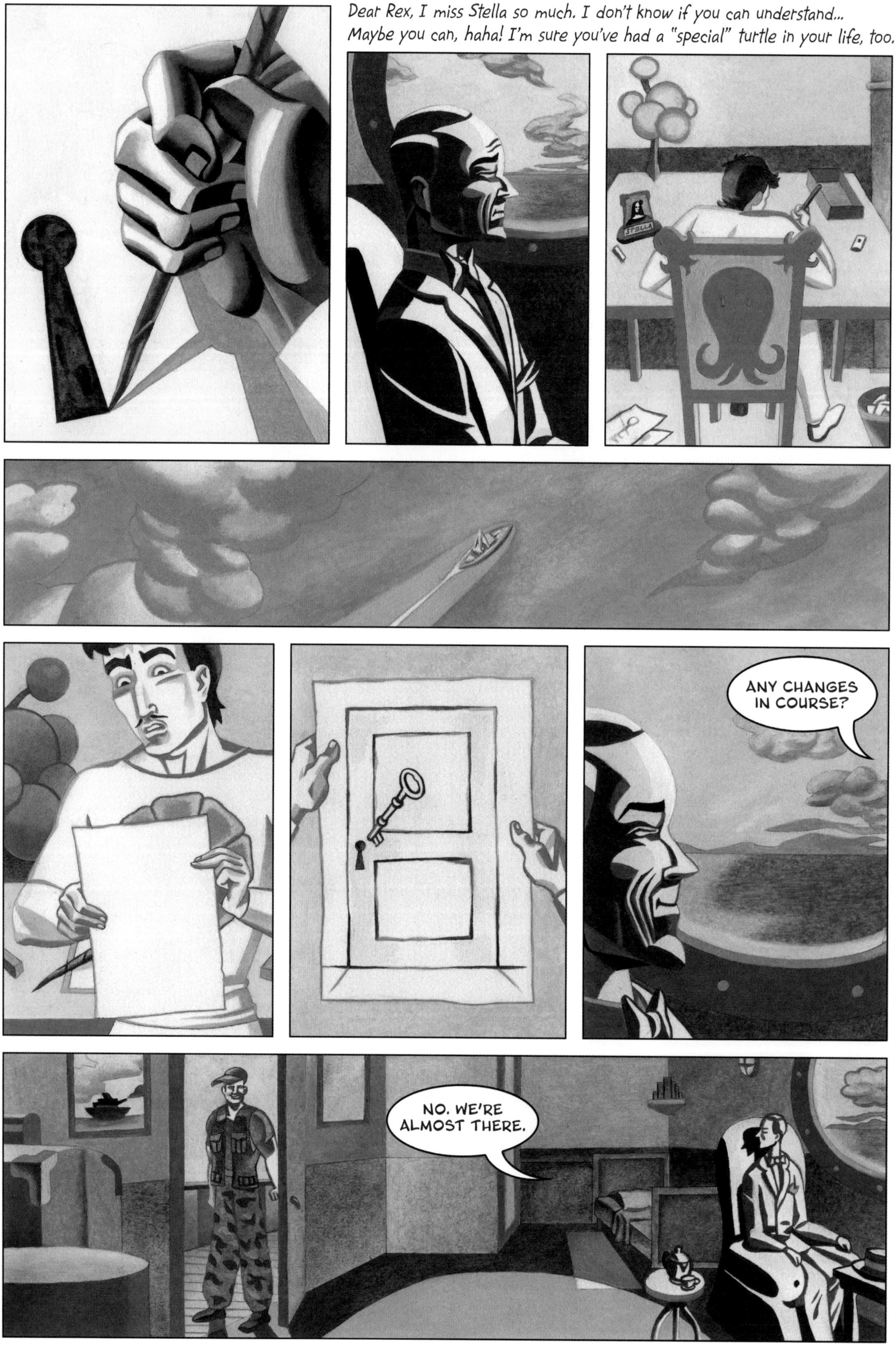
Dear Rex, I miss Stella so much. I don't know if you can understand...
Maybe you can, haha! I'm sure you've had a "special" turtle in your life, too.
ANY CHANGES IN COURSE?
NO. WE'RE ALMOST THERE.

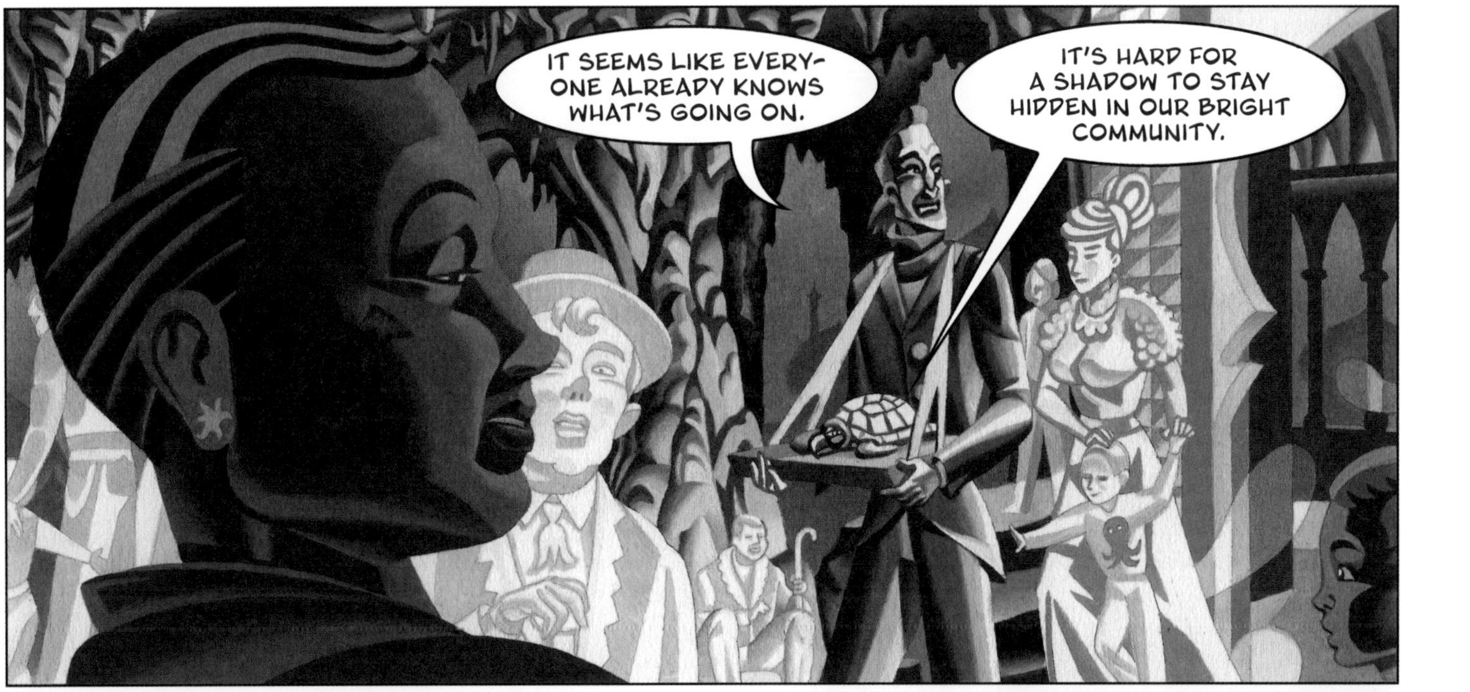
IT SEEMS LIKE EVERY-ONE ALREADY KNOWS WHAT'S GOING ON.
IT'S HARD FOR A SHADOW TO STAY HIDDEN IN OUR BRIGHT COMMUNITY.

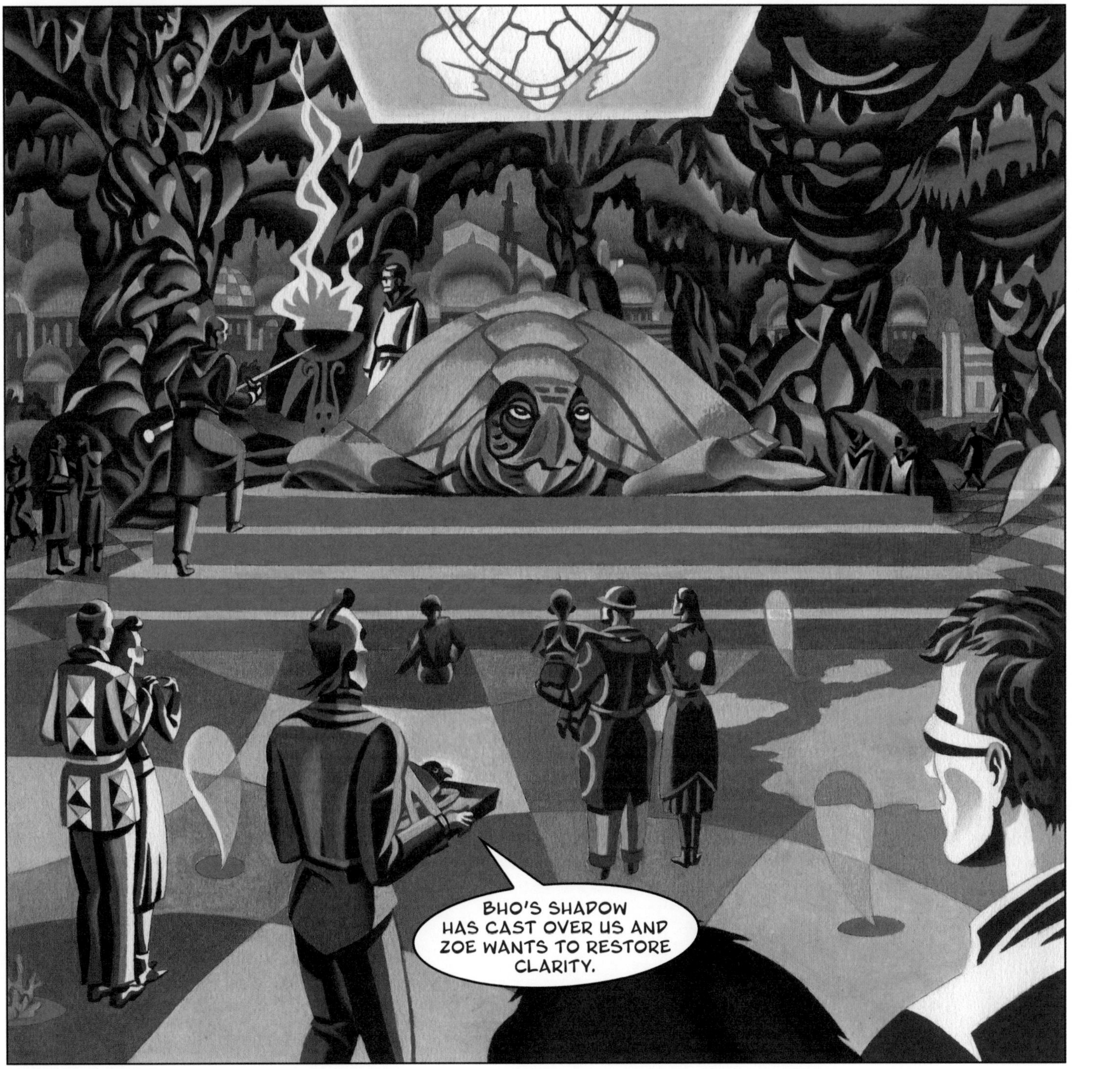
BHO'S SHADOW HAS CAST OVER US AND ZOE WANTS TO RESTORE CLARITY.

I'LL NEVER GET USED TO THIS TORTURE.
FOR ZOE, THE SHELL ORACLE, TO LIGHT OUR PATH, PAIN IS BUT A SMALL PRICE TO PAY.
SORRY TO CORRECT YOU, LITTLE FRIEND...
BUT HAVING A RED-HOT SPINDLE STUCK BETWEEN THE SCUTES IS A PRICE THAT COMES PRETTY CLOSE TO TORTURE...
YOU'RE RIGHT, HOWEVER...
TODAY, OUR COMMUNITY NEEDS MY SUFFERING.
AN IMAGE IS STARTING TO FORM.

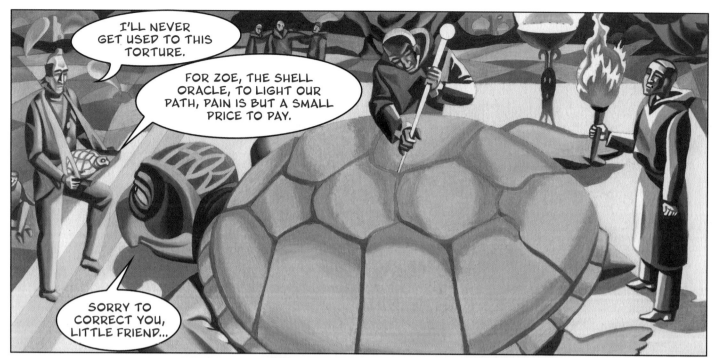

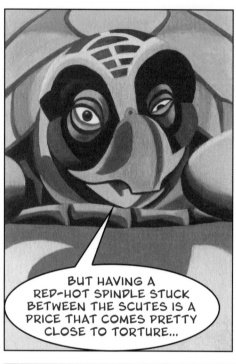

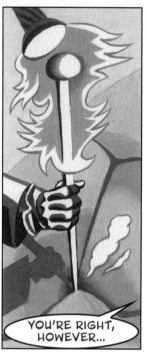

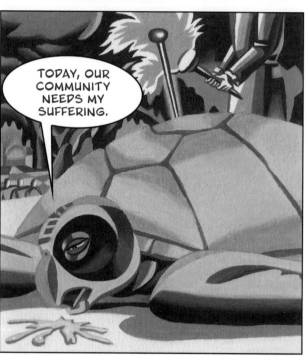

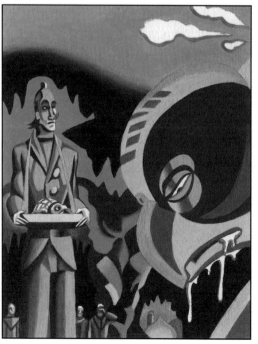

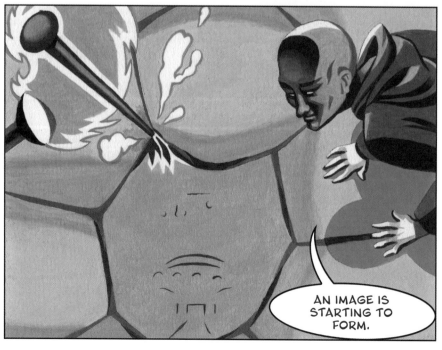

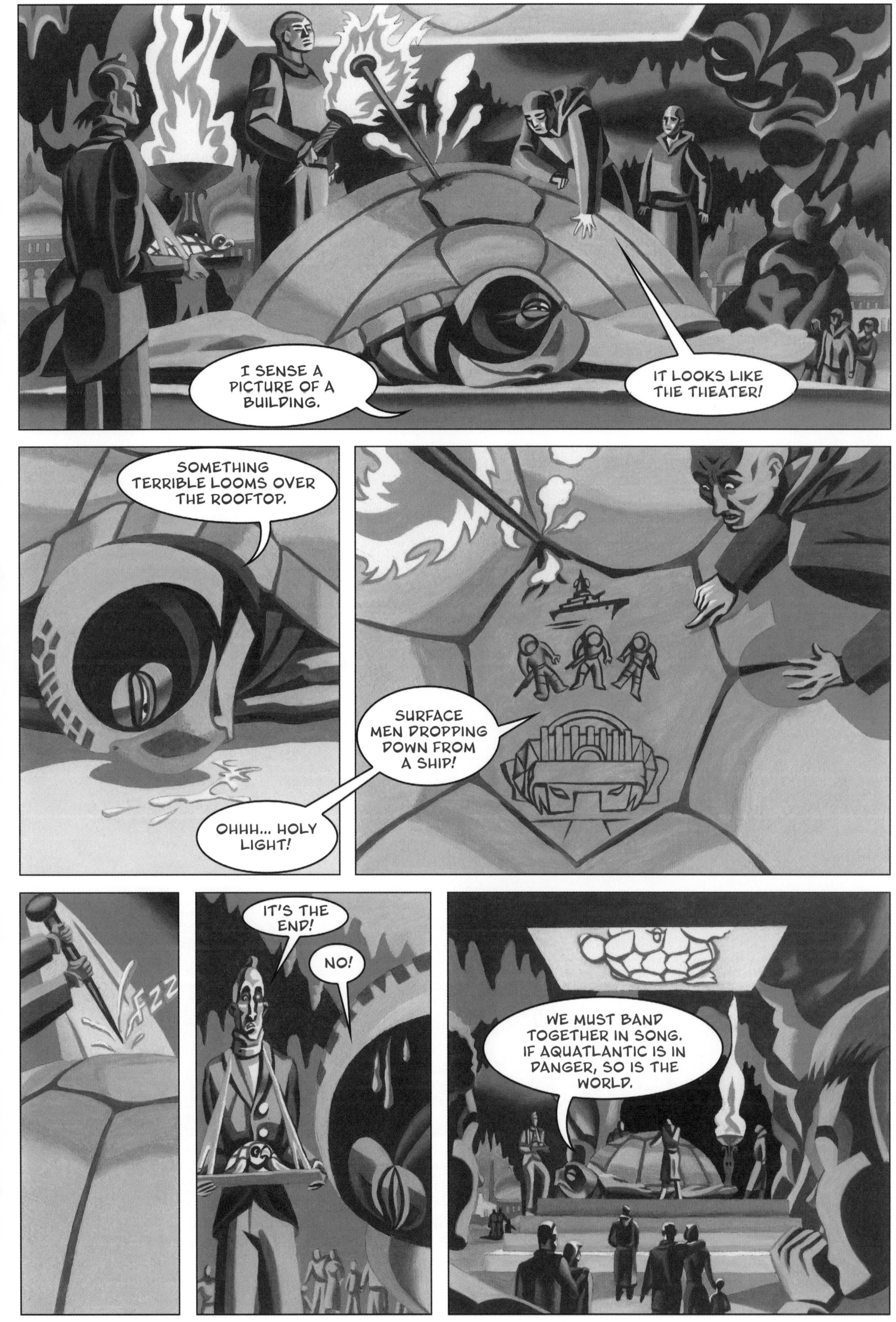
I SENSE A PICTURE OF A BUILDING.
IT LOOKS LIKE THE THEATER!
SOMETHING TERRIBLE LOOMS OVER THE ROOFTOP.
SURFACE MEN DROPPING DOWN FROM A SHIP!
OHHH... HOLY LIGHT!
FZZ
IT'S THE END!
NO!
WE MUST BAND TOGETHER IN SONG. IF AQUATLANTIC IS IN DANGER, SO IS THE WORLD.

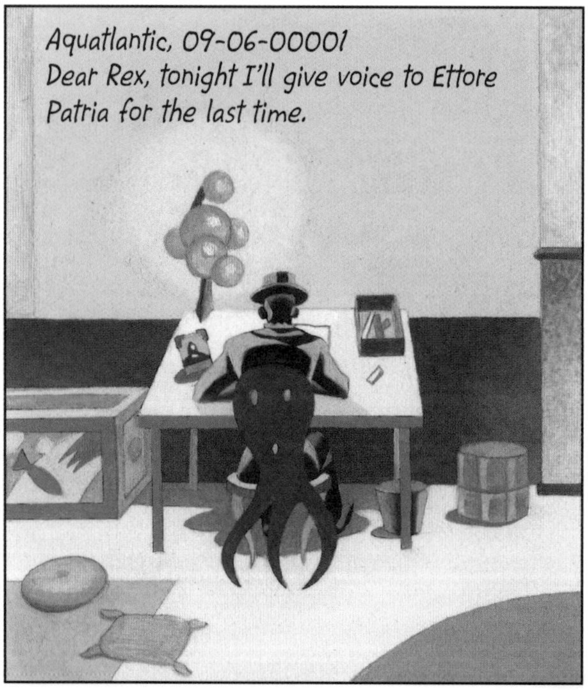
Aquatlantic, 09-06-00001
Dear Rex, tonight I'll give voice to Ettore Patria for the last time.

Last show. The end, good night! I'll have to come up with something else... Maybe a musical about you turtles. What do you say, would you like a part?

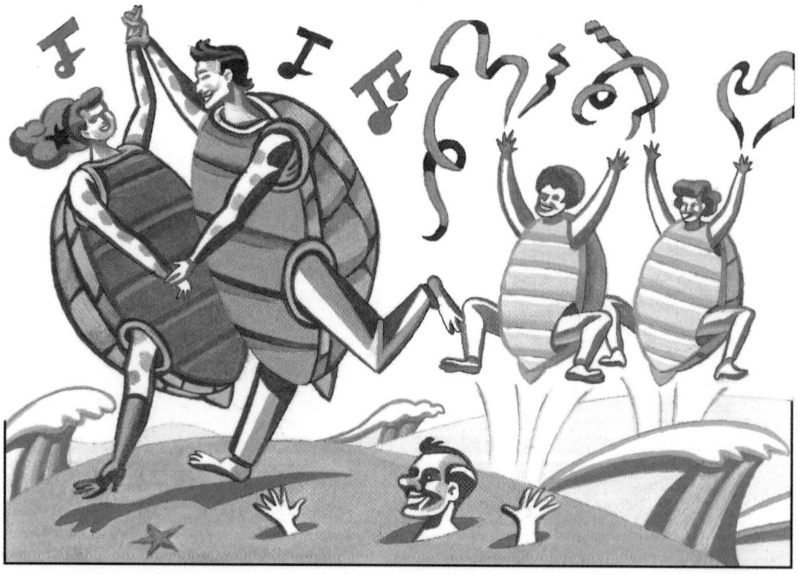

It's just a thought. We'll see.

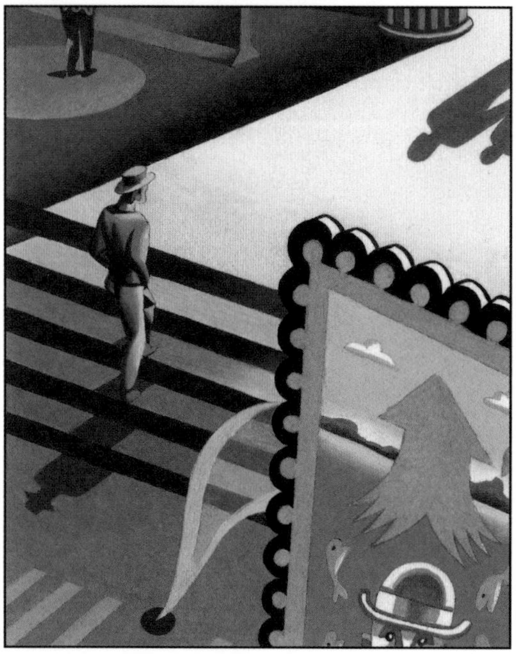

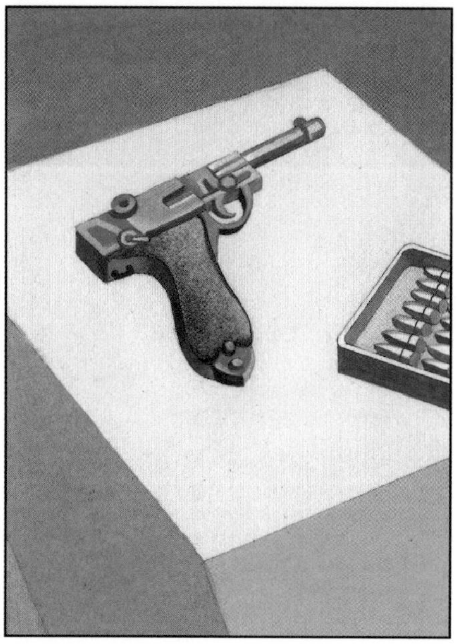

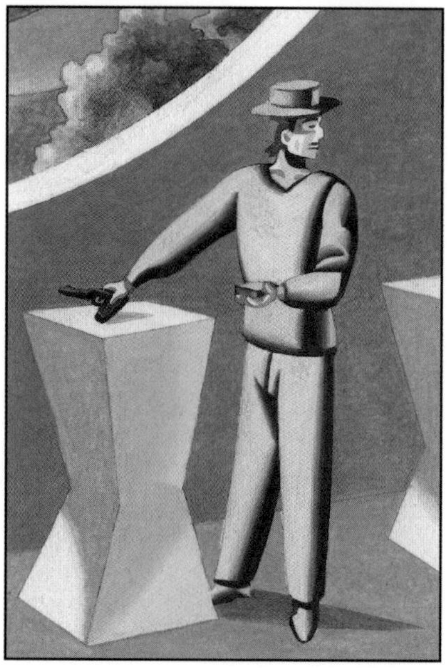

Anyway, it'll be a relief to be free of "him." At this point I have his voice in my head even off stage.

Maybe I haven't told you, but that's what worries me: sometimes it's like I'm sleepwalking...

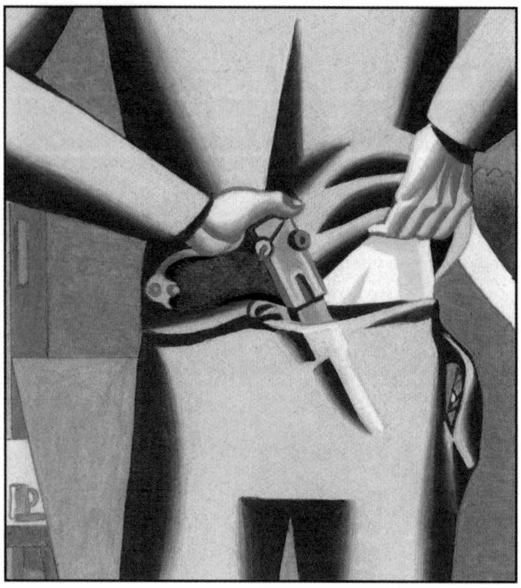

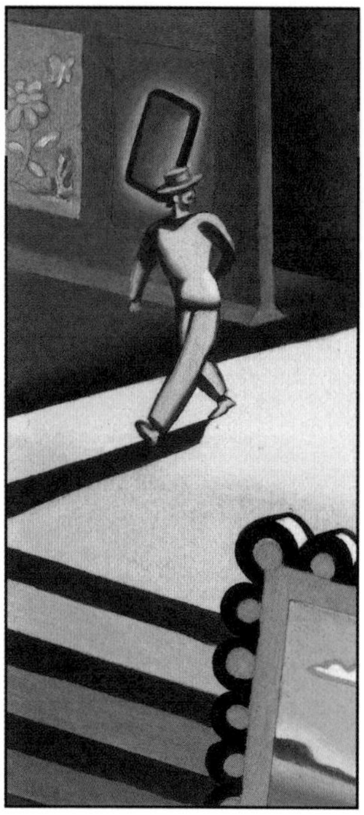

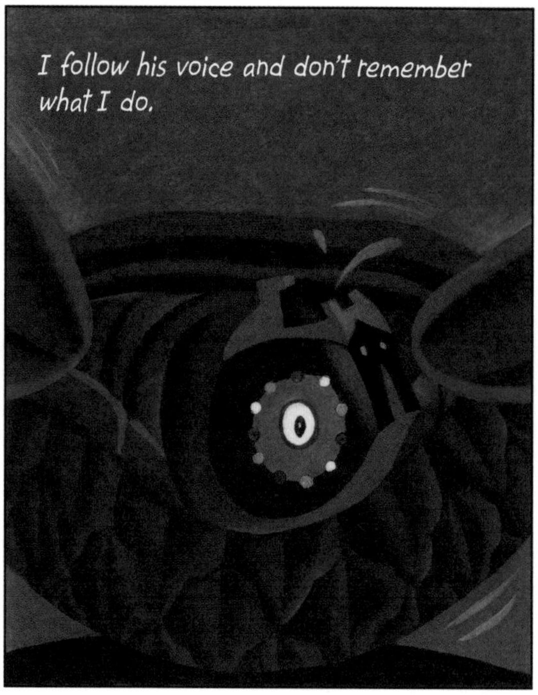
I follow his voice and don't remember what I do.

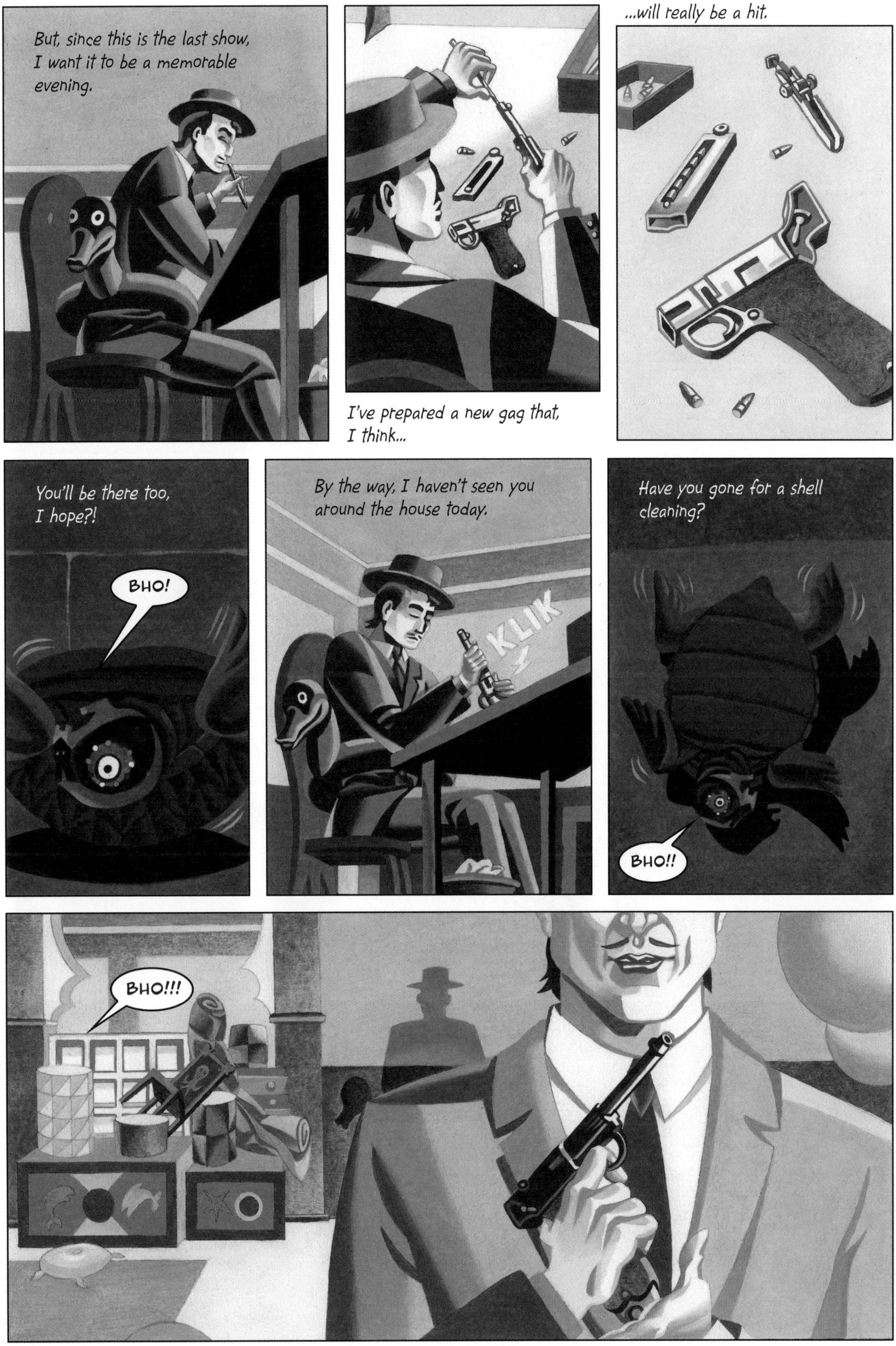

But, since this is the last show, I want it to be a memorable evening.
I've prepared a new gag that, I think...
...will really be a hit.
You'll be there too, I hope?!
BHO!
By the way, I haven't seen you around the house today.
KLIK
Have you gone for a shell cleaning?
BHO!!
BHO!!!

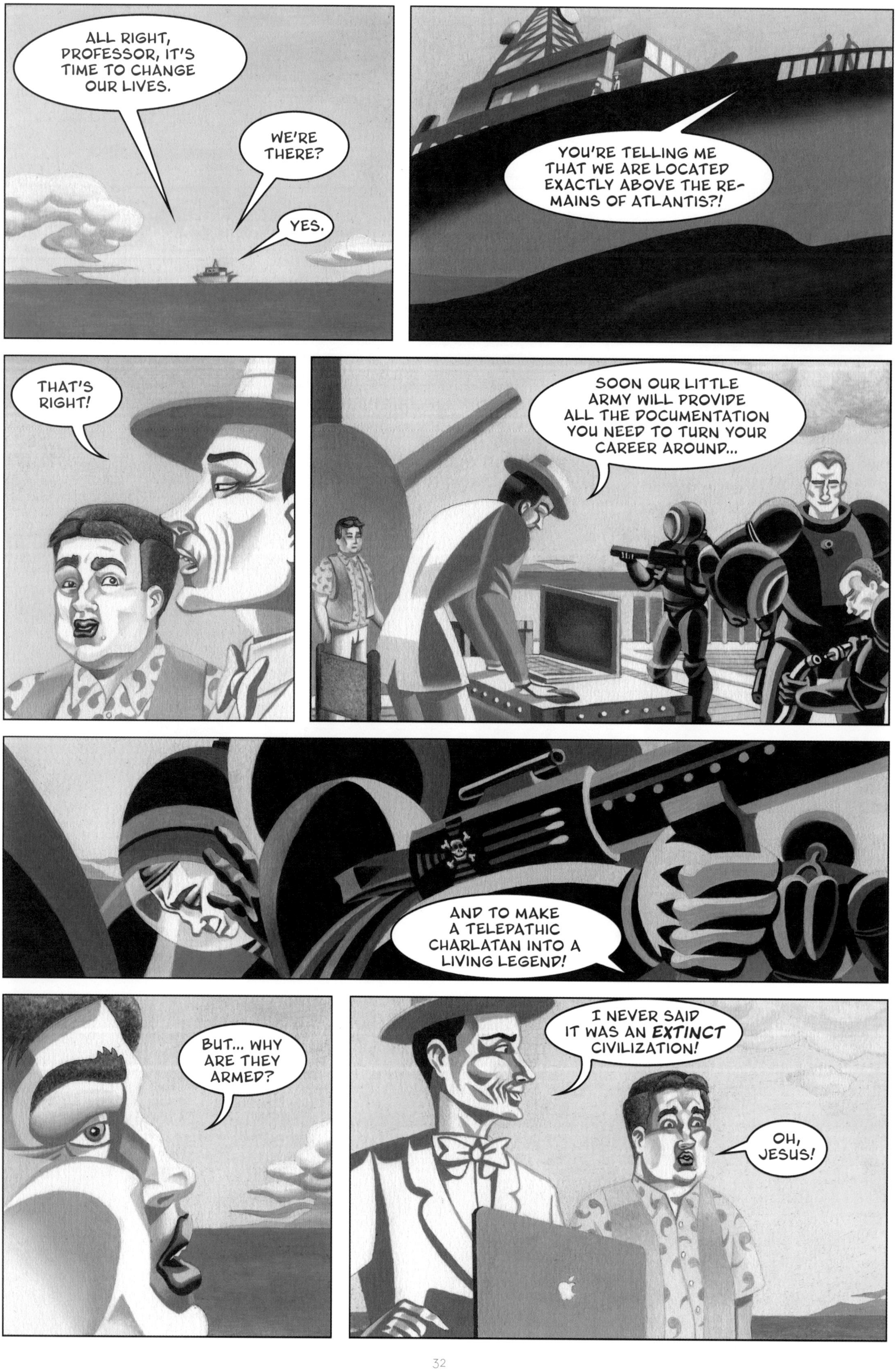
ALL RIGHT, PROFESSOR, IT'S TIME TO CHANGE OUR LIVES.
WE'RE THERE?
YES.
YOU'RE TELLING ME THAT WE ARE LOCATED EXACTLY ABOVE THE RE-MAINS OF ATLANTIS?!
THAT'S RIGHT!
SOON OUR LITTLE ARMY WILL PROVIDE ALL THE DOCUMENTATION YOU NEED TO TURN YOUR CAREER AROUND...
AND TO MAKE A TELEPATHIC CHARLATAN INTO A LIVING LEGEND!
BUT... WHY ARE THEY ARMED?
I NEVER SAID IT WAS AN EXTINCT CIVILIZATION!
OH, JESUS!

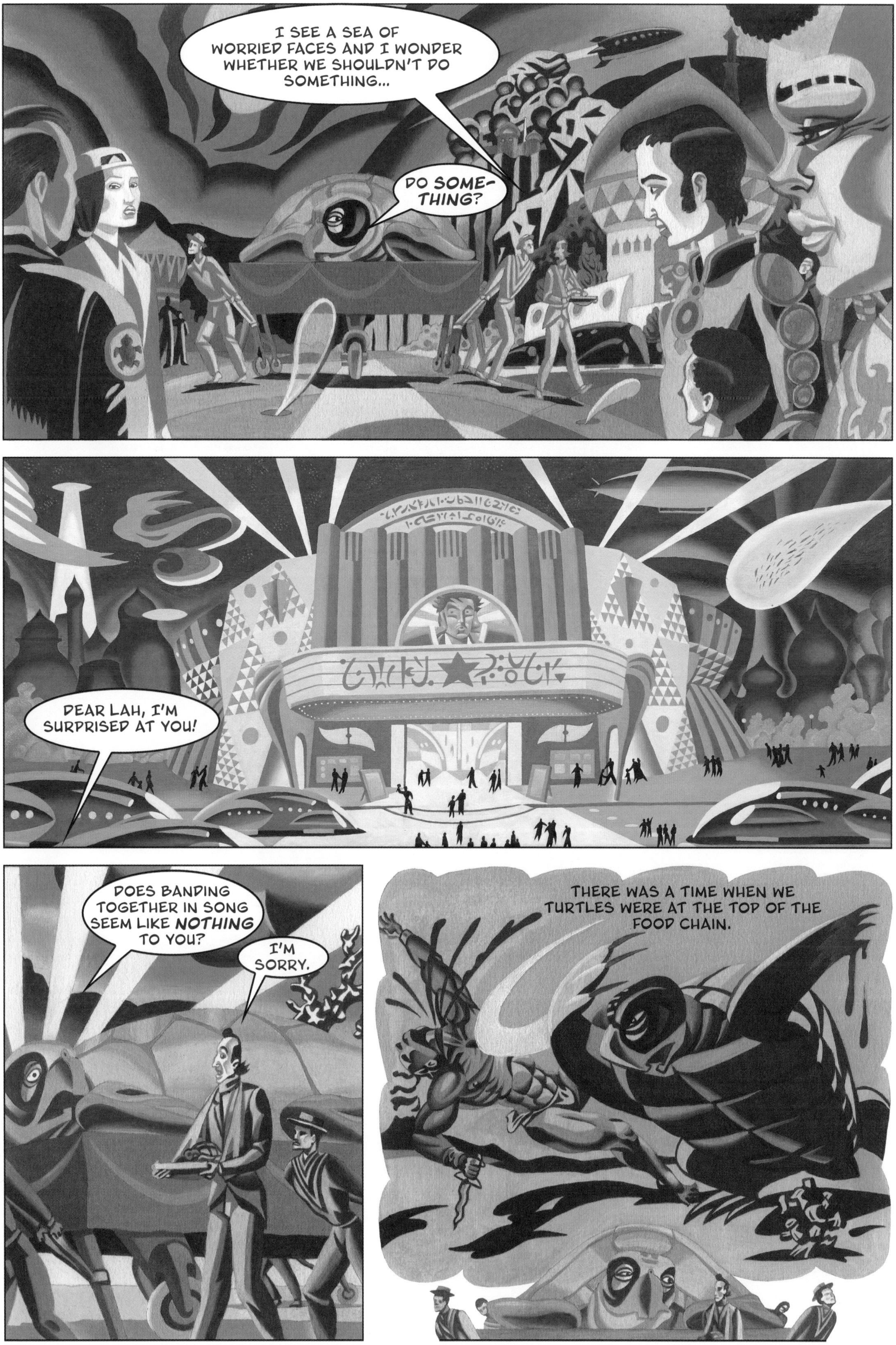
I SEE A SEA OF WORRIED FACES AND I WONDER WHETHER WE SHOULDN'T DO SOMETHING...
DO SOME-THING?
DEAR LAH, I'M SURPRISED AT YOU!
DOES BANDING TOGETHER IN SONG SEEM LIKE NOTHING TO YOU?
I'M SORRY.
THERE WAS A TIME WHEN WE TURTLES WERE AT THE TOP OF THE FOOD CHAIN.

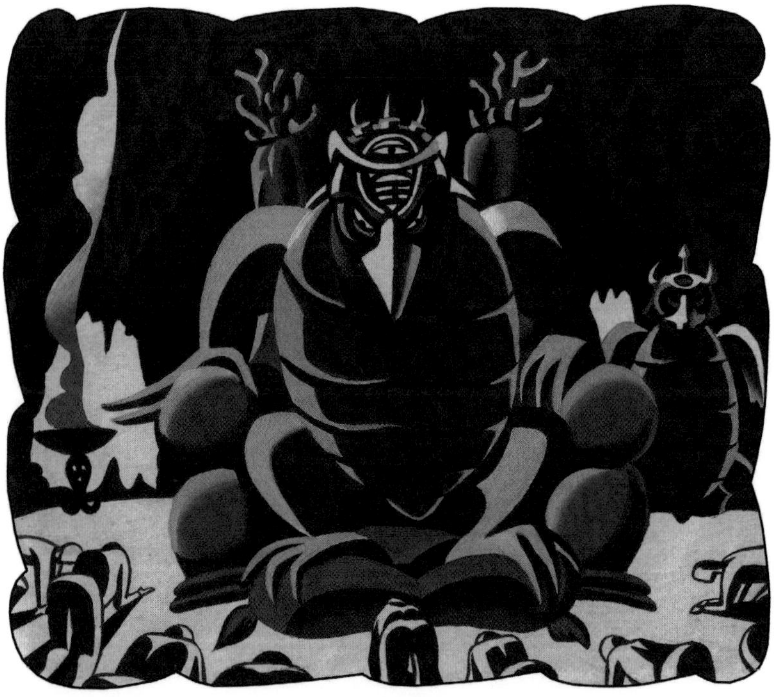

WE COULD HAVE CONTROLLED THE WORLD, BUT INSTEAD WE DECIDED TO CONTROL OURSELVES.

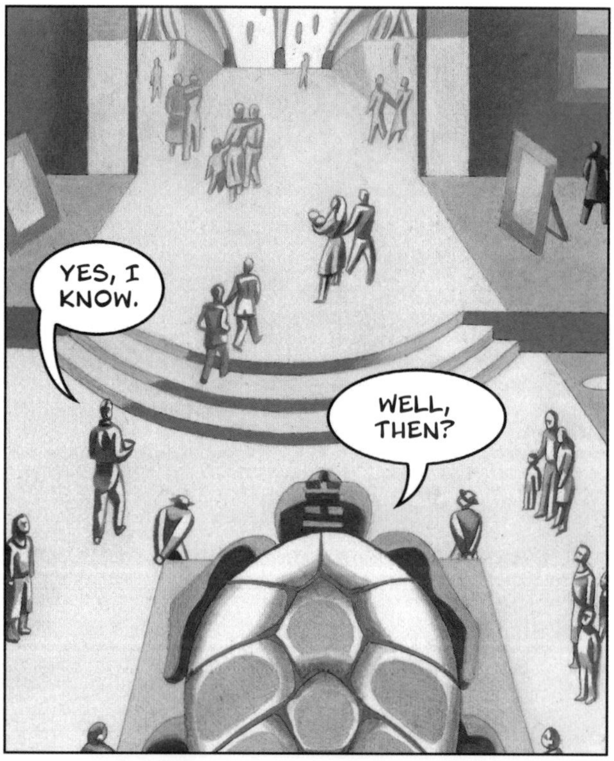
YES, I KNOW.
WELL, THEN?

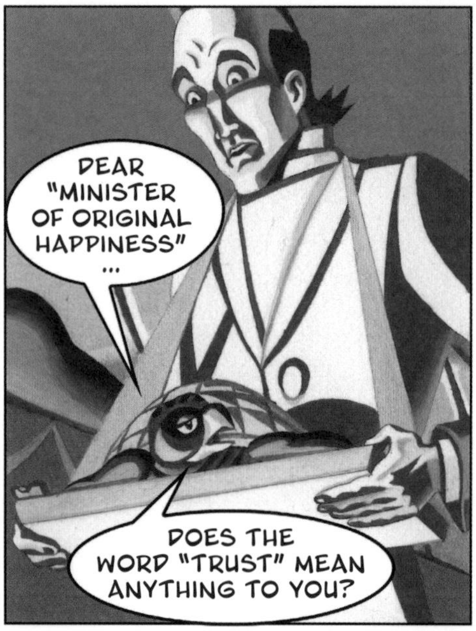
DEAR "MINISTER OF ORIGINAL HAPPINESS" ...
DOES THE WORD "TRUST" MEAN ANYTHING TO YOU?

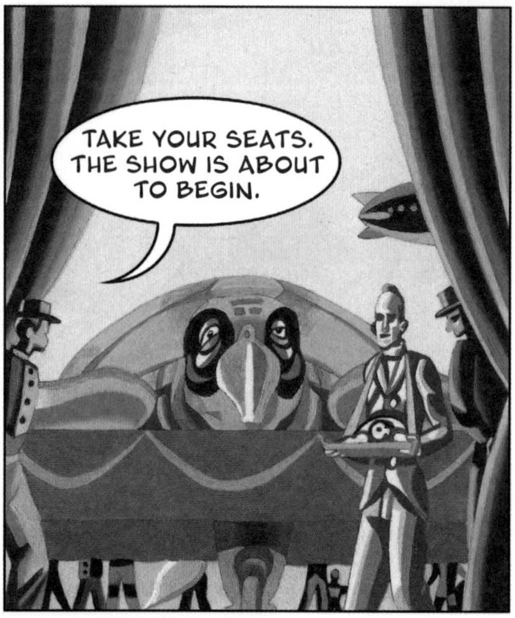
TAKE YOUR SEATS. THE SHOW IS ABOUT TO BEGIN.

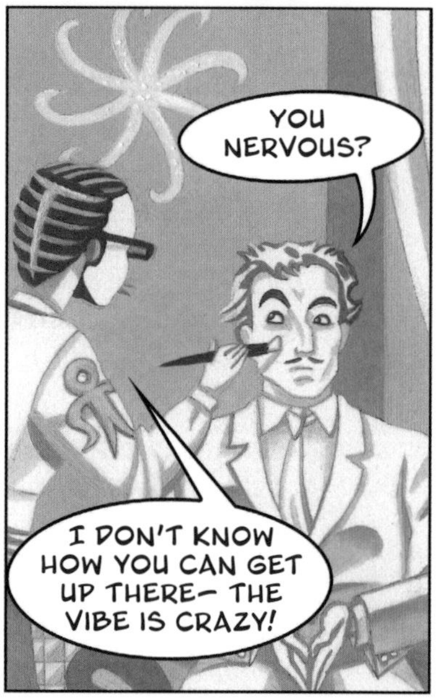
YOU NERVOUS?
I DON'T KNOW HOW YOU CAN GET UP THERE– THE VIBE IS CRAZY!

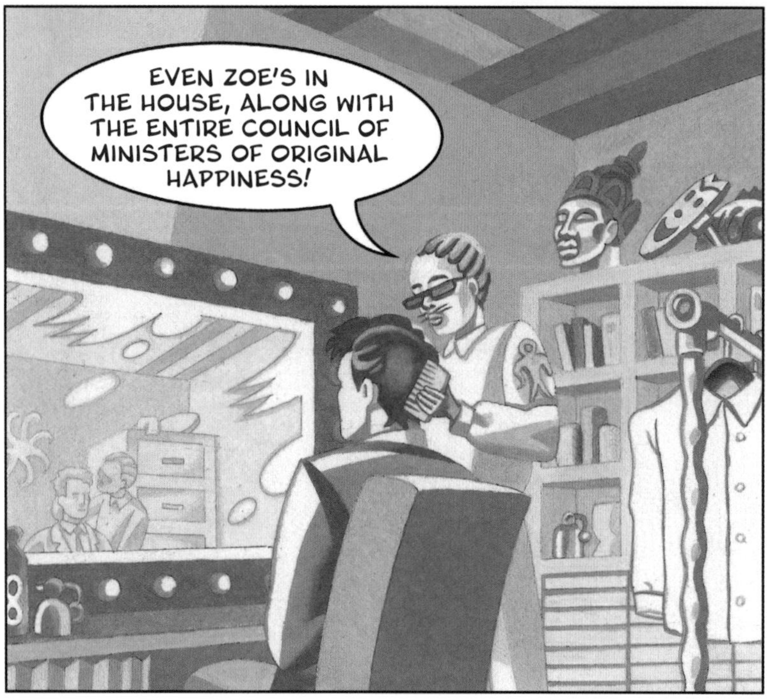
EVEN ZOE'S IN THE HOUSE, ALONG WITH THE ENTIRE COUNCIL OF MINISTERS OF ORIGINAL HAPPINESS!

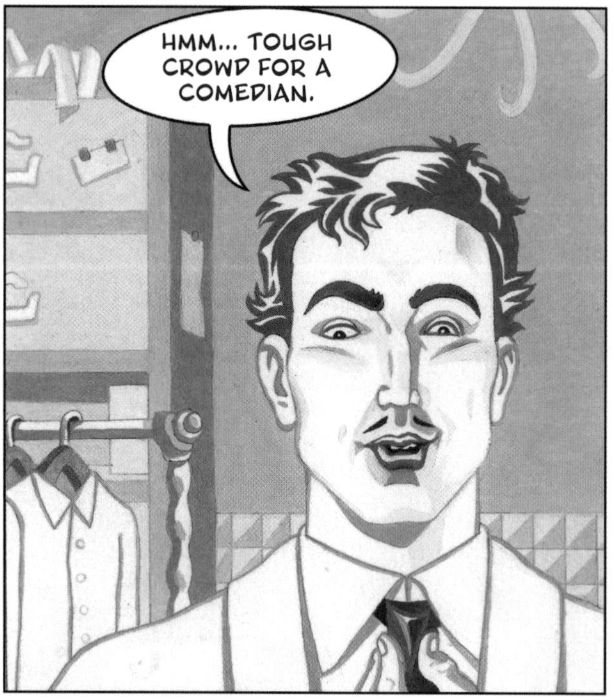
HMM... TOUGH CROWD FOR A COMEDIAN.

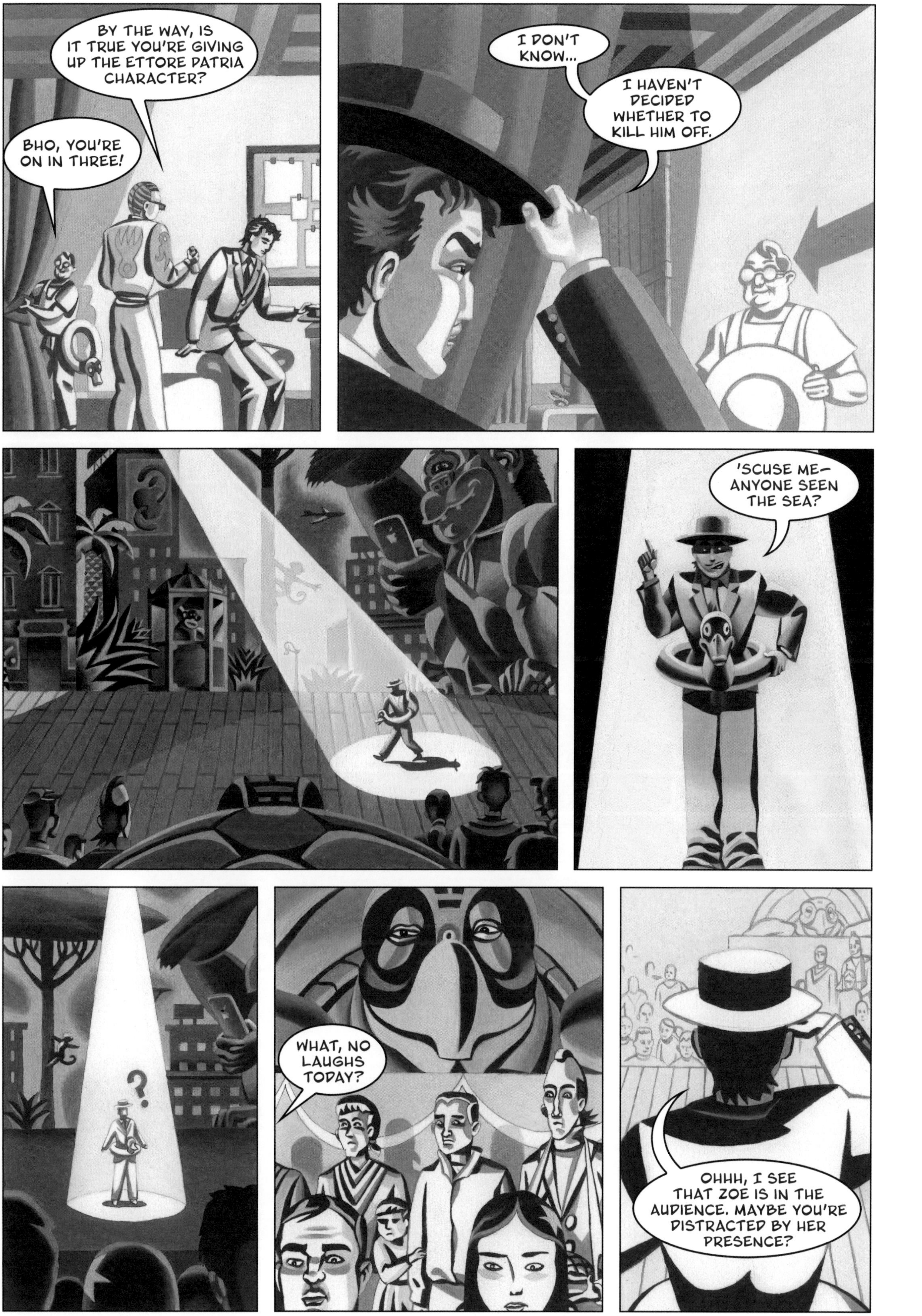
BY THE WAY, IS IT TRUE YOU'RE GIVING UP THE ETTORE PATRIA CHARACTER?
BHO, YOU'RE ON IN THREE!
I DON'T KNOW...
I HAVEN'T DECIDED WHETHER TO KILL HIM OFF.
'SCUSE ME— ANYONE SEEN THE SEA?
?
WHAT, NO LAUGHS TODAY?
OHHH, I SEE THAT ZOE IS IN THE AUDIENCE. MAYBE YOU'RE DISTRACTED BY HER PRESENCE?

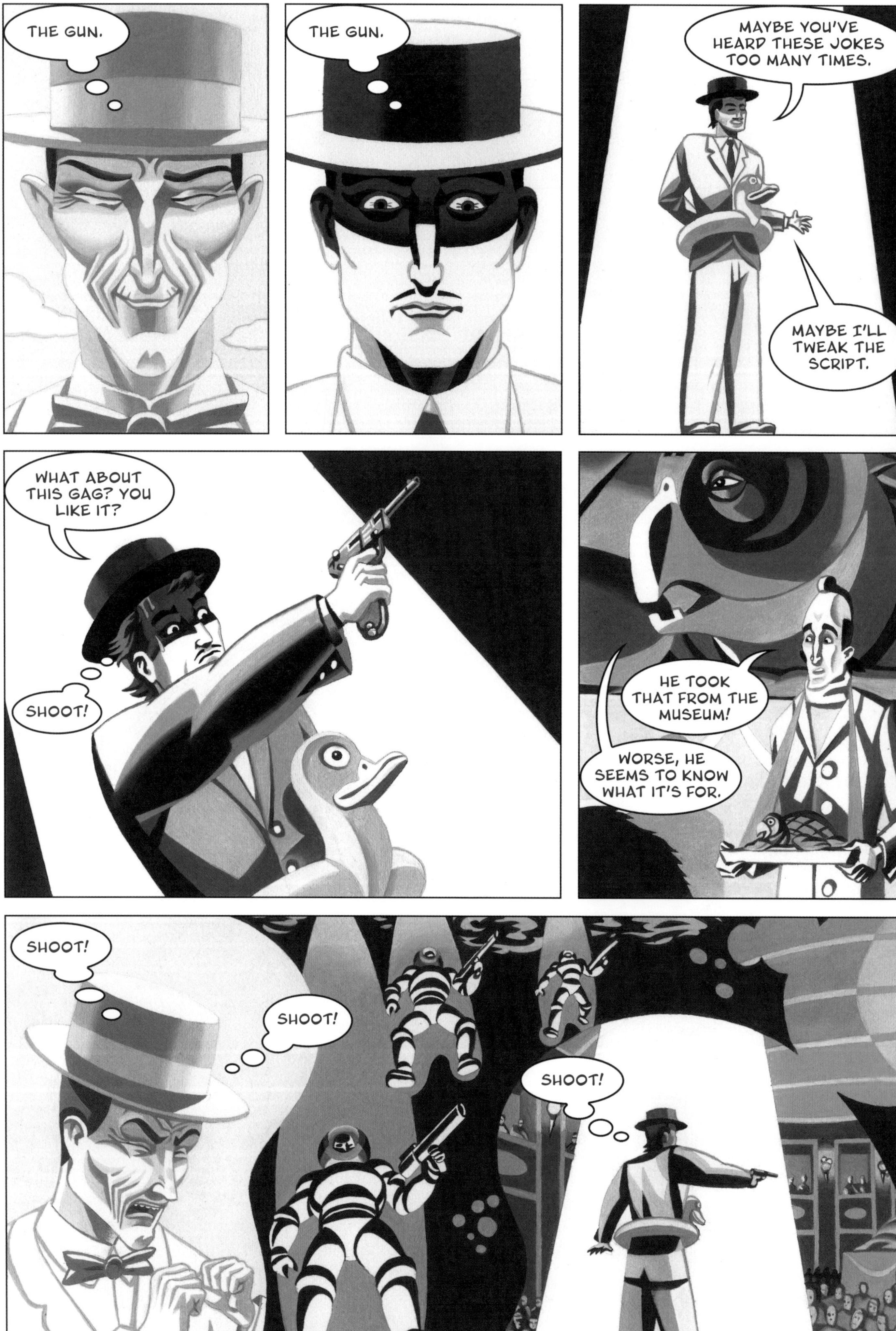
THE GUN.
THE GUN.
MAYBE YOU'VE HEARD THESE JOKES TOO MANY TIMES.
MAYBE I'LL TWEAK THE SCRIPT.
WHAT ABOUT THIS GAG? YOU LIKE IT?
SHOOT!
HE TOOK THAT FROM THE MUSEUM!
WORSE, HE SEEMS TO KNOW WHAT IT'S FOR.
SHOOT!
SHOOT!
SHOOT!

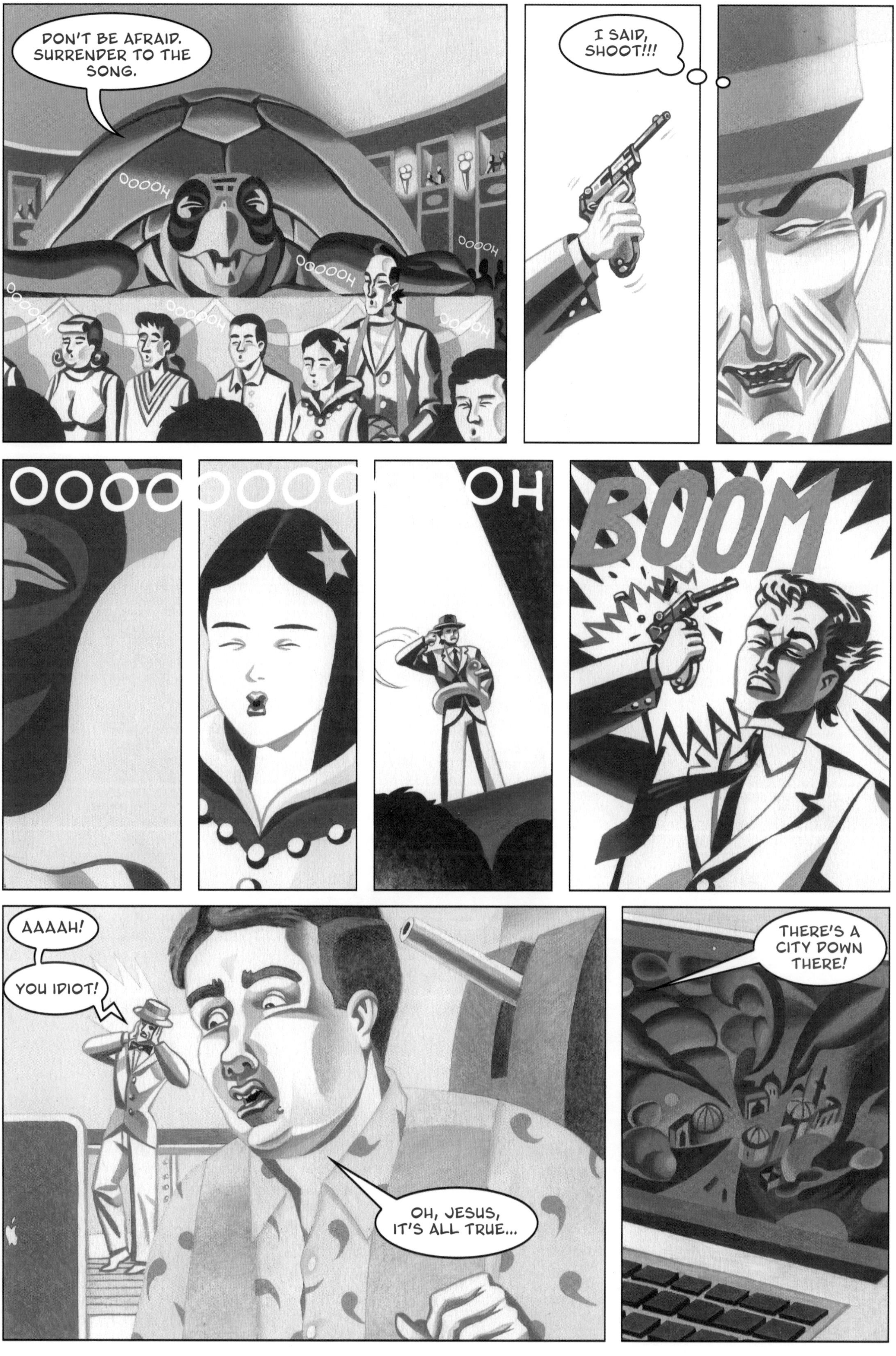

DON'T BE AFRAID. SURRENDER TO THE SONG.
OOOOH
OOOOH
OOOOOH
OOOOOH
OOOOOH
OOOOH
I SAID, SHOOT!!!
OOOOOOOOOOOOOOOH
BOOM
AAAAH!
YOU IDIOT!
OH, JESUS, IT'S ALL TRUE...
THERE'S A CITY DOWN THERE!

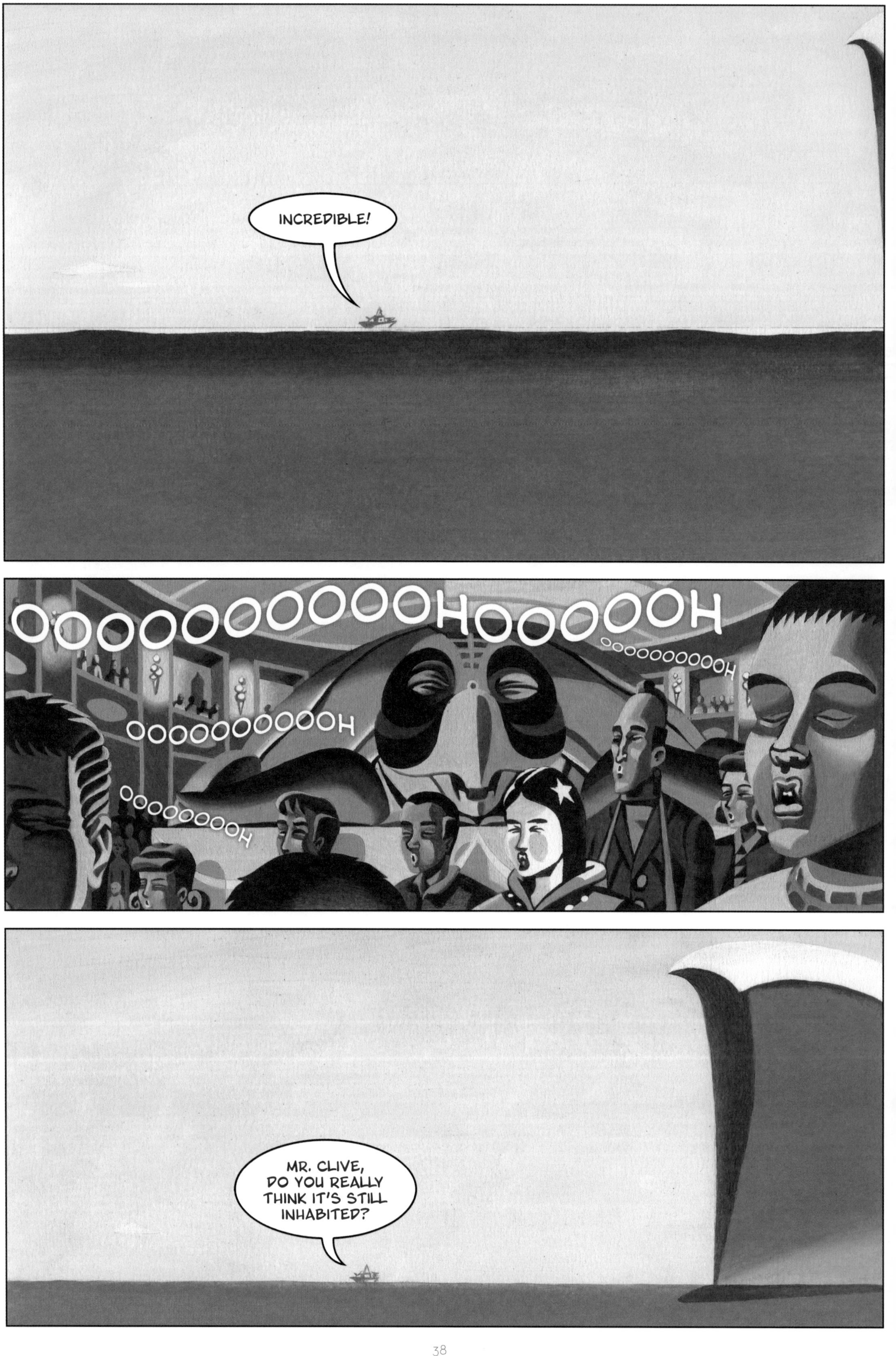
INCREDIBLE!
OOOOOOOOOOHOOOOOH
OOOOOOOOOOOH
OOOOOOOOOOH
OOOOOOOOOH
MR. CLIVE, DO YOU REALLY THINK IT'S STILL INHABITED?

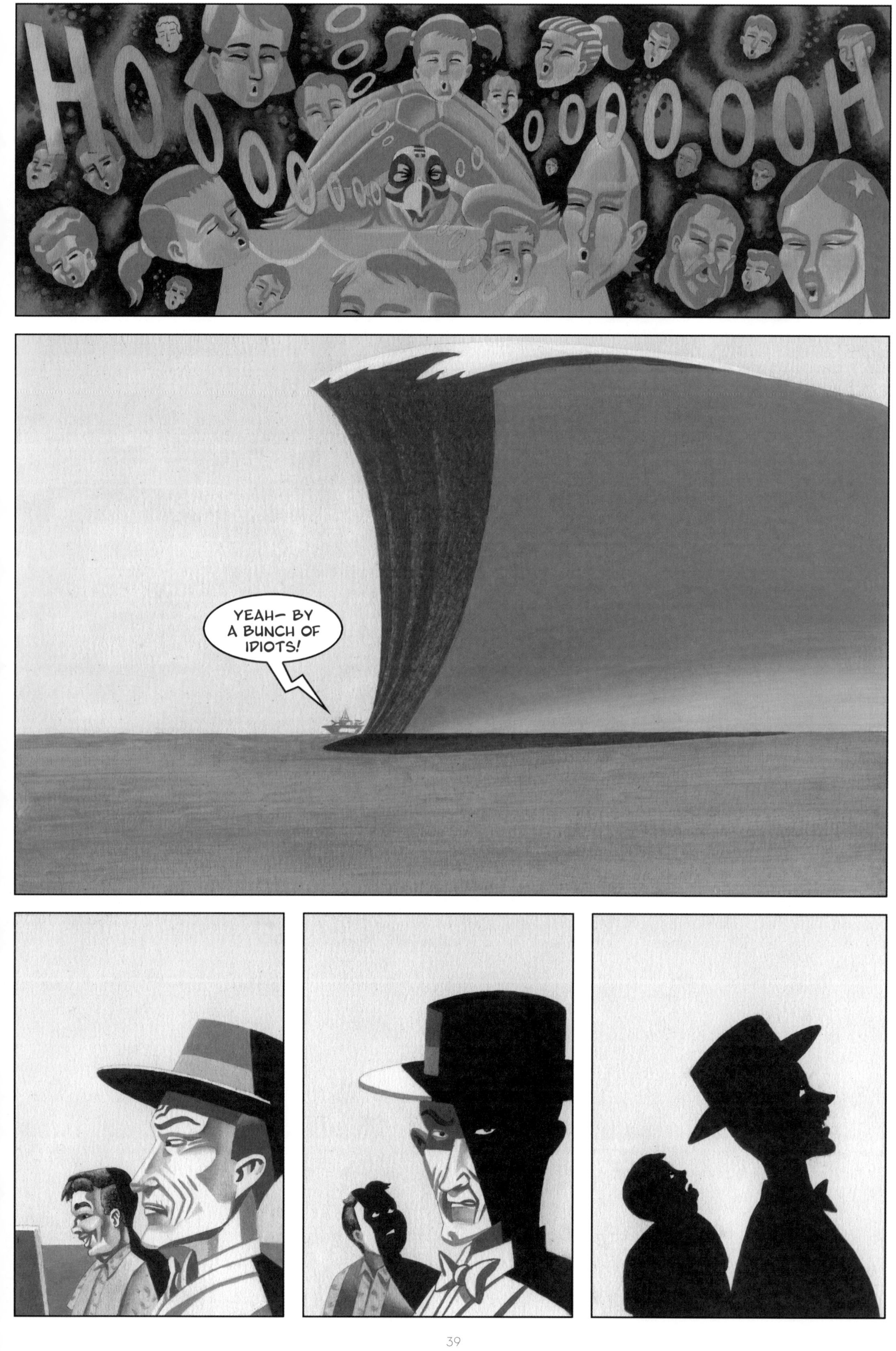
HOOOOOOOOOOOOOOOOH
YEAH— BY A BUNCH OF IDIOTS!

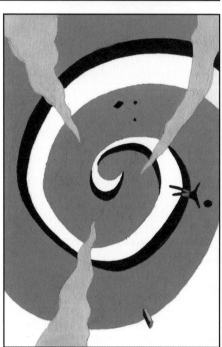

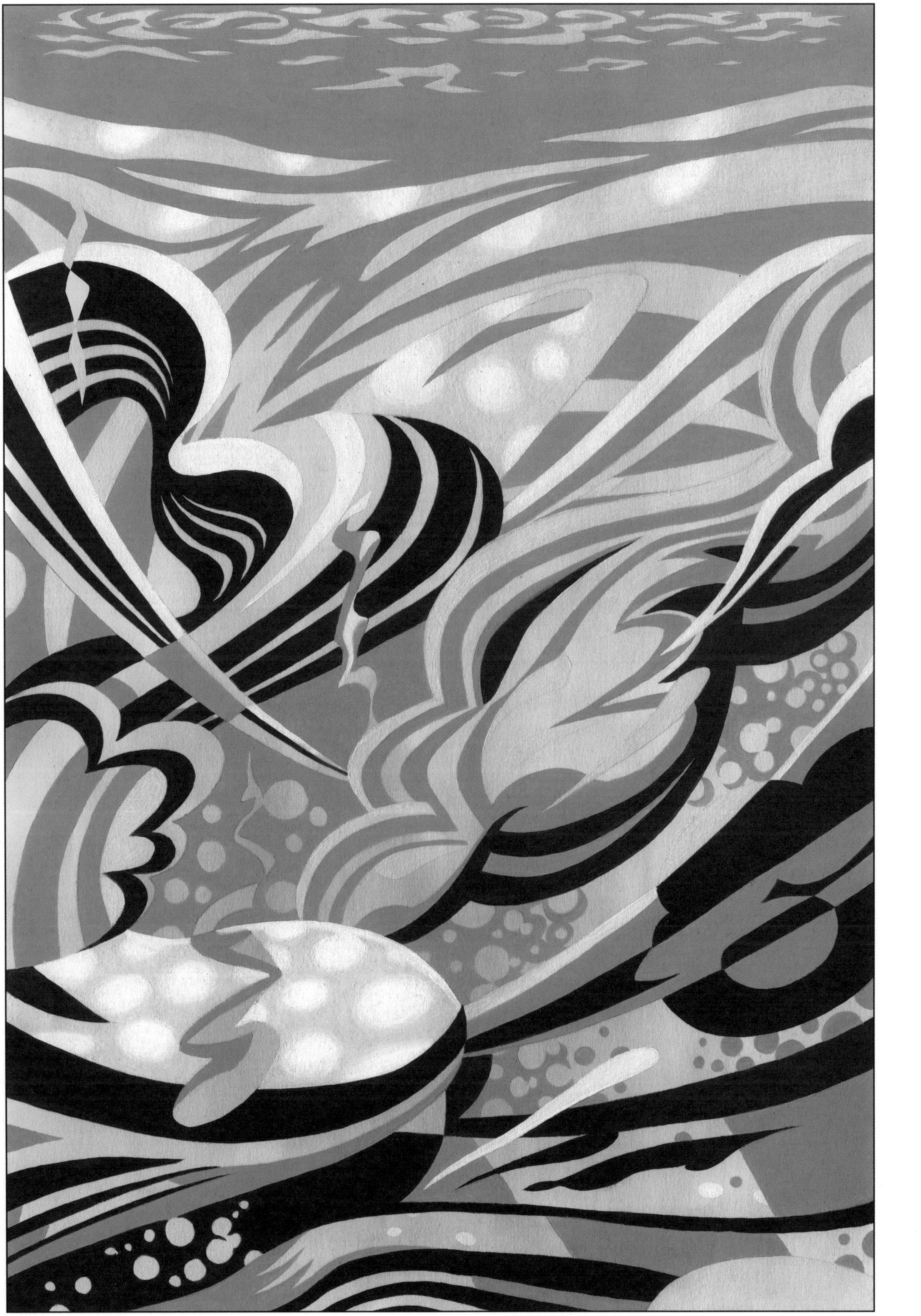

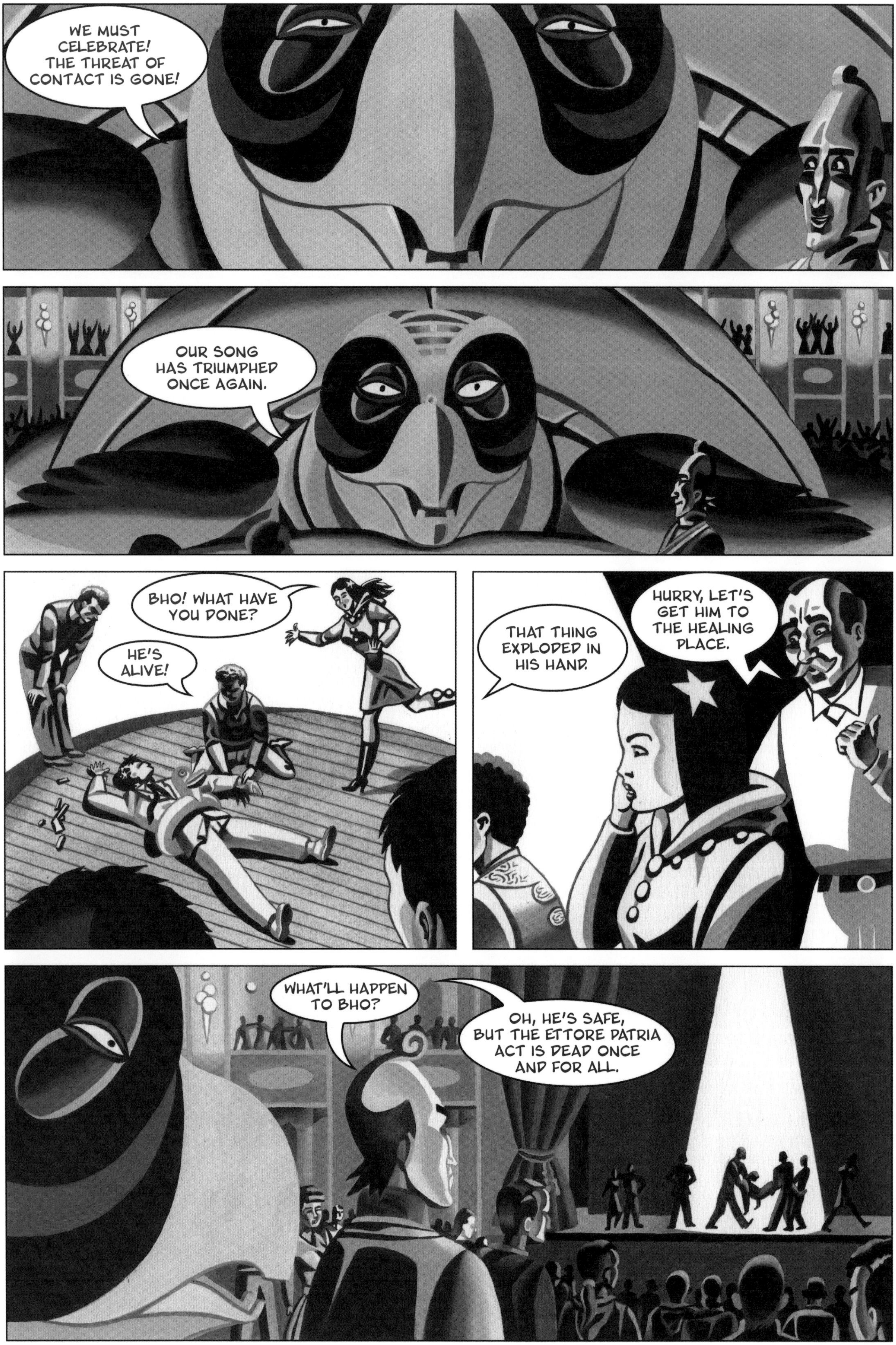
WE MUST CELEBRATE! THE THREAT OF CONTACT IS GONE!
OUR SONG HAS TRIUMPHED ONCE AGAIN.
BHO! WHAT HAVE YOU DONE?
HE'S ALIVE!
THAT THING EXPLODED IN HIS HAND.
HURRY, LET'S GET HIM TO THE HEALING PLACE.
WHAT'LL HAPPEN TO BHO?
OH, HE'S SAFE, BUT THE ETTORE PATRIA ACT IS DEAD ONCE AND FOR ALL.

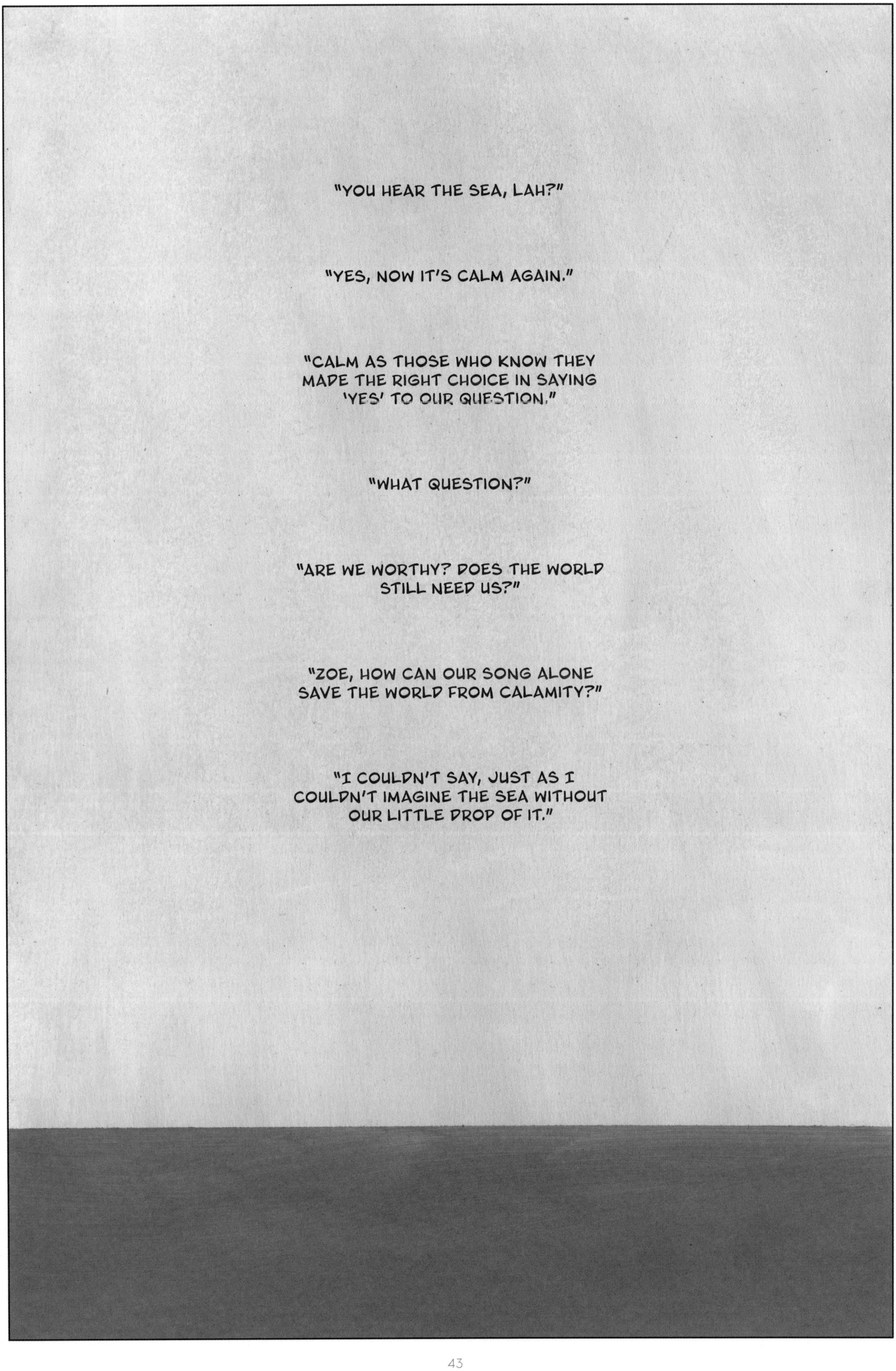
"YOU HEAR THE SEA, LAH?"
"YES, NOW IT'S CALM AGAIN."
"CALM AS THOSE WHO KNOW THEY MADE THE RIGHT CHOICE IN SAYING 'YES' TO OUR QUESTION."
"WHAT QUESTION?"
"ARE WE WORTHY? DOES THE WORLD STILL NEED US?"
"ZOE, HOW CAN OUR SONG ALONE SAVE THE WORLD FROM CALAMITY?"
"I COULDN'T SAY, JUST AS I COULDN'T IMAGINE THE SEA WITHOUT OUR LITTLE DROP OF IT."

Aquatlantic, 32-06-00001

Dear Rex, I think I need to ask forgiveness from a list as long as the population of Aquatlantic. First on the list is Stella, but you're number two. I had that voice in my head that, well... You've already heard all about it.

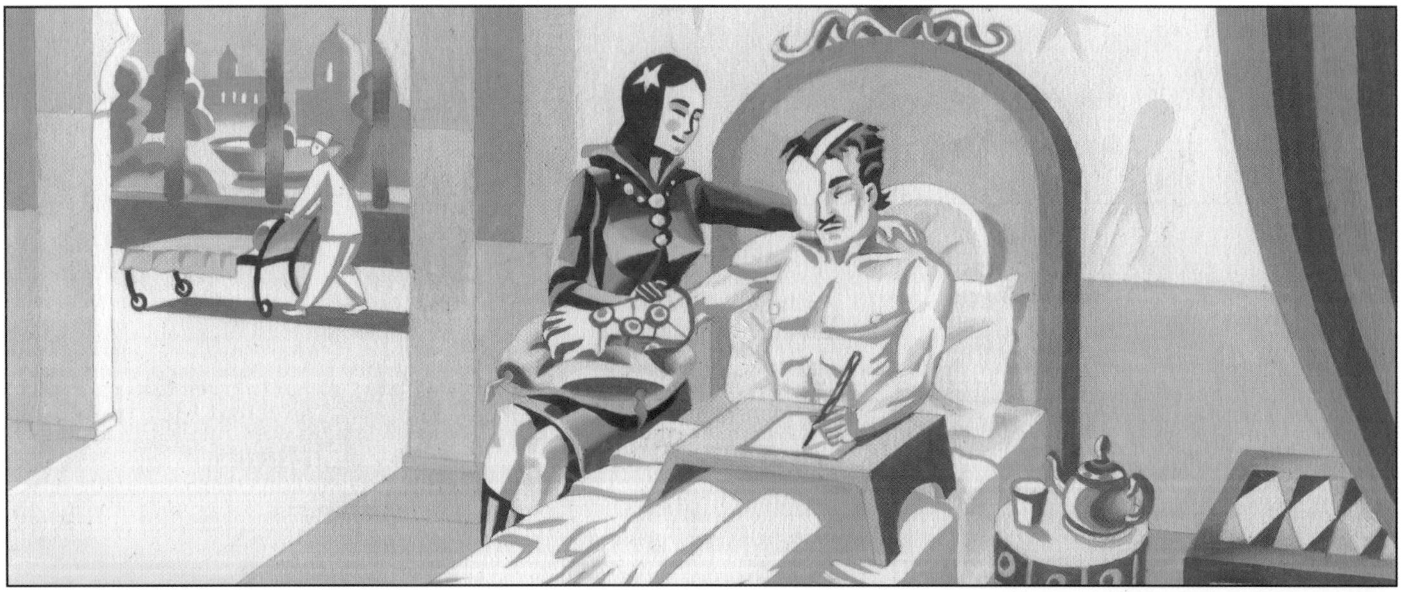

I still can't believe I turned you on your back...
it must have been...

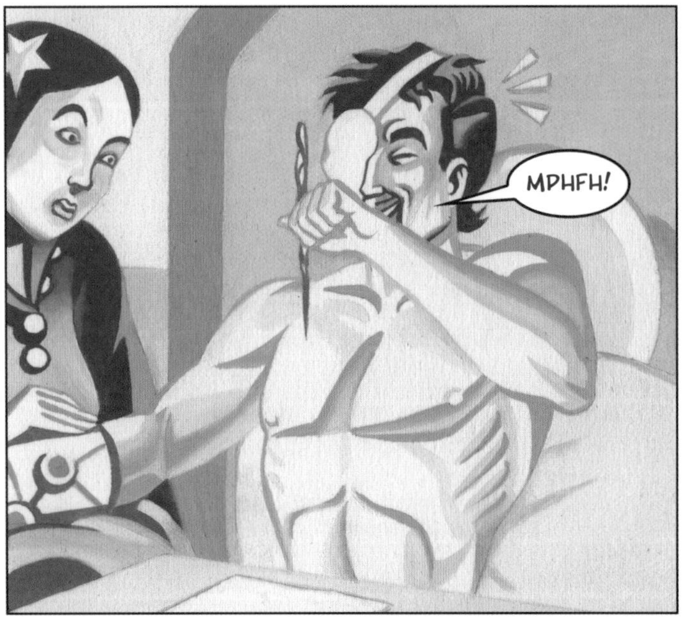
MPHFH!

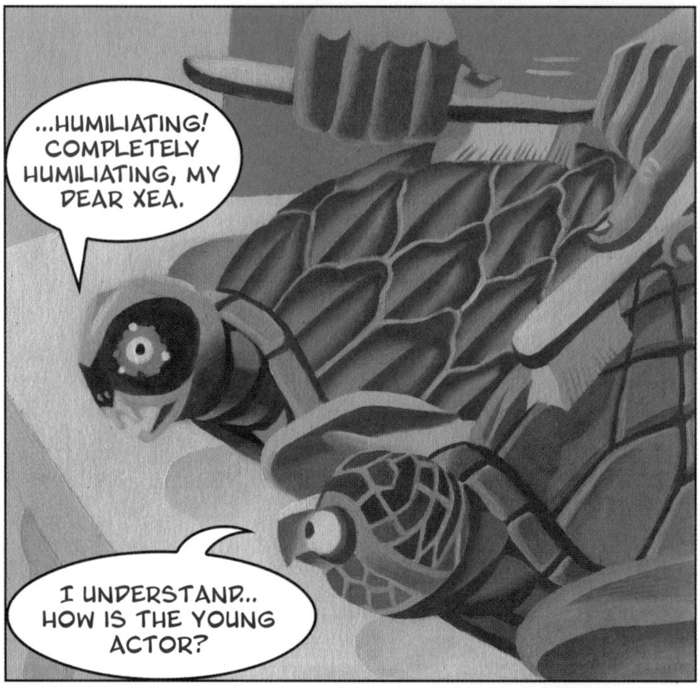
...HUMILIATING! COMPLETELY HUMILIATING, MY DEAR XEA.
I UNDERSTAND... HOW IS THE YOUNG ACTOR?

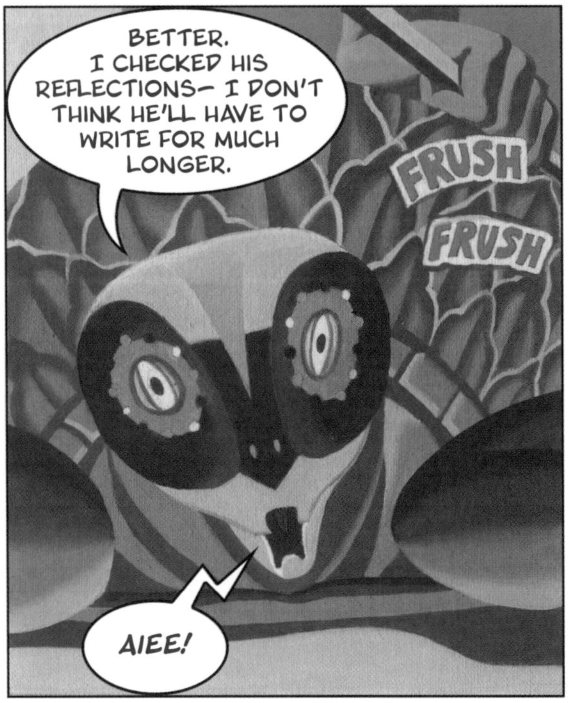
BETTER. I CHECKED HIS REFLECTIONS— I DON'T THINK HE'LL HAVE TO WRITE FOR MUCH LONGER.
FRUSH
FRUSH
AIEE!

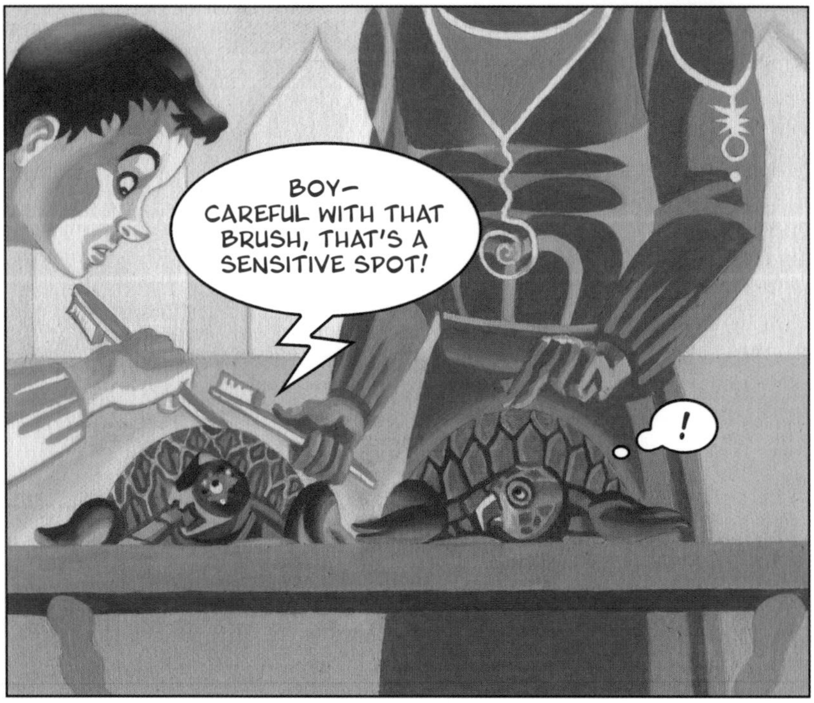
BOY— CAREFUL WITH THAT BRUSH, THAT'S A SENSITIVE SPOT!
!

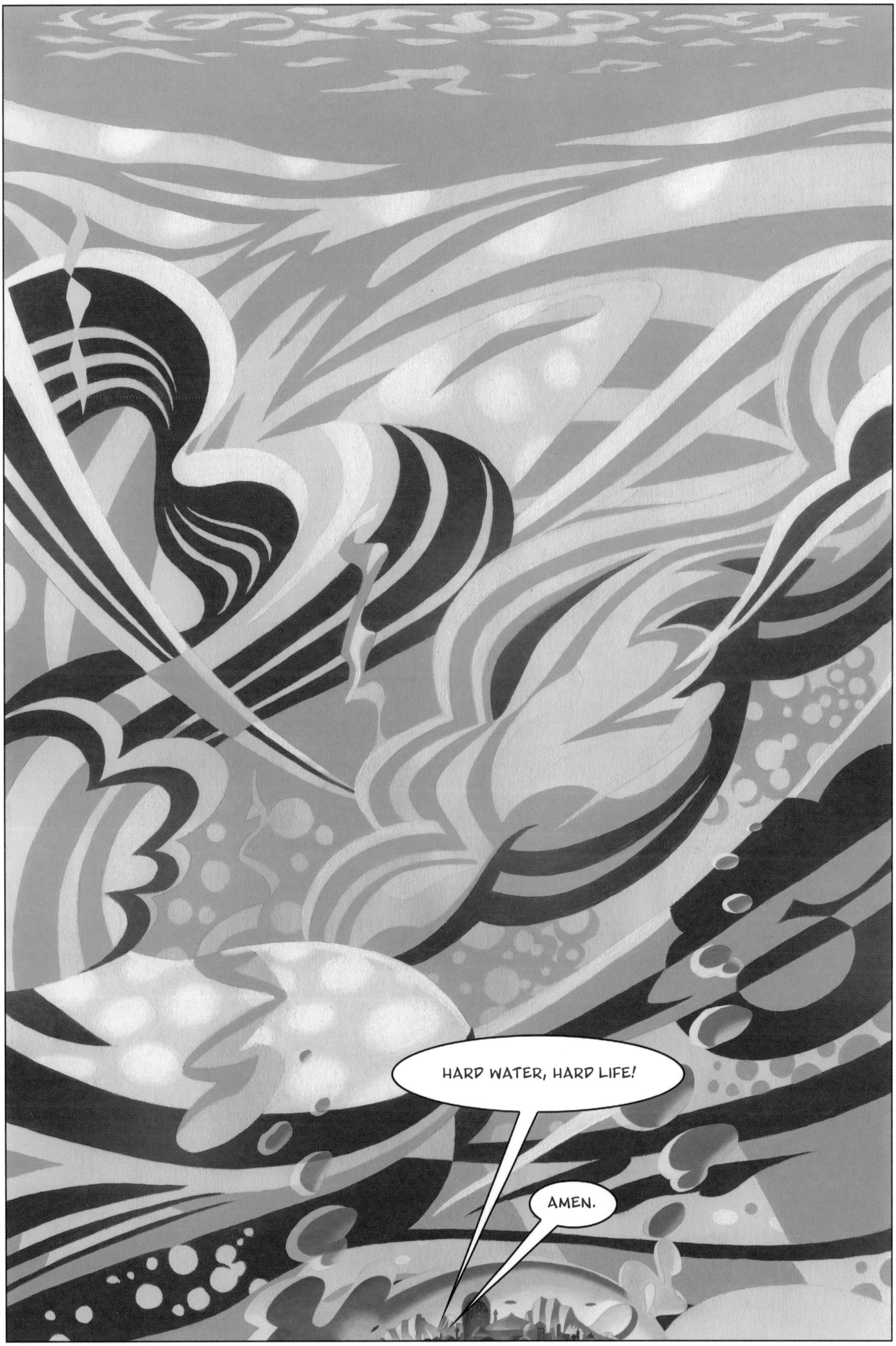
HARD WATER, HARD LIFE!
AMEN.

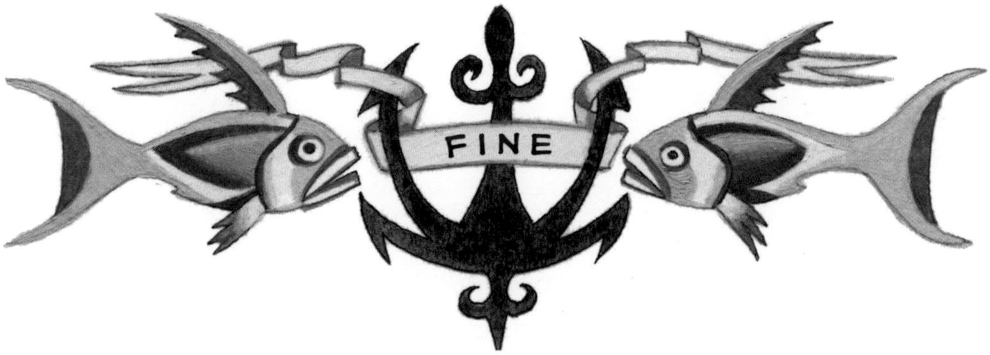
FINE

# AFTERWORD

I've always had an Olympic disinterest in anything having to do with the myth of Atlantis. Apart from the beautiful name, I've always found it a very boring and ultra-retro subject.

Then I woke up one day and found myself developing a story that called for an "other" place. Somewhere far from the commotion of our technological trinkets. A small corner of the universe where our civilization originated.

After months of working on the story, I still wasn't sure why I had chosen the sea floor as its setting. Sure, the deep sea recalls the emergence of life... our origins. Of course, submarine life is certainly an "elsewhere" compared to our habitat on the earth's surface. Not to mention the implications of the distinction between "superficial" and "deep," conscious and unconscious. Fine. I realized that Atlantis had come to my aid as a setting for my story, but to me, Atlantis still meant "boring." Then, with the help of a tech trinket called YouTube, I saw a clip from a BBC documentary on a Japanese puffer fish. In that video, something vibrated at the same frequency as my story idea and this something swept any lingering doubts about my choice. Perhaps that "boredom" was only a cloud of prejudice hiding something beautiful and vital.

The video shows the fish tracing a bas-relief on the seabed where it lived. The work required an entire week, excluding sleeping and eating. It "sculpted" the drawing with its belly and its nose, adding some final touches with shells set down with its mouth.

Charles Burns

48

The director follows its work, persistently and meticulously, in close-ups that save a vision of the whole for the final scene: it is a round mandala, complex and sunlike. In the voice over, the ichthyology expert states that a puffer fish might make this design in order to attract a female partner. Even if that were so, the fact remains that a little fish is doing a big job, at the limits of its ability, to foster the continuation of the species.

An act of faith for the greatest gift one can imagine. In a time as disillusioned as ours, finding something that has remained "beautiful and vital" at the bottom of our hearts is a discovery as worthy as a Nobel, and with a little ingenuity, determination, and sacrifice, one we can all make.

—GIORGIO CARPINTERI

**THANKS TO**

*Charles Burns, Igort,
and Lorenzo Mattotti, for each
contributing a drawing to this book.
Orsola Mattioli, Dimitri Moretti,
and last but not least, my wife
Maria Cristina.*